Do I Really H*te Men?

Giving Hope to the Journey of Divorce and Parenting

Ang Allan-Burns

Do I Really H*te Men?: Giving Hope to the Journey of Divorce and Parenting
©2024 Angela Diane Allan-Burns

All rights reserved. No part of this book may be reproduced, stored in a retrieval system or transmitted in any form or by any means (electronic, mechanical, photocopy, recording, scanning or other) except for brief quotations in critical reviews or articles, without the prior written permission of the publisher.

ISBN: 9781068789106 Paperback

Published by: Inspired By Publishing

The strategies outlined in this book are provided primarily for educational purposes. Every effort has been made to trace the copyright holders and obtain their permission for the use of copyright material.

The information and resources provided in this book are based on the author's personal experiences. As such, any outcomes or results described are specific to the author and may not be indicative of your own experience. There is no guarantee that you will achieve similar results after reading this book.

This book is not intended to replace professional medical care or advice. Always seek the advice of a doctor or qualified mental health professional if you have any concerns about your mental or physical health.

The author reserves the right to make changes to the content and assumes no responsibility or liability for any actions taken by purchasers or readers of this material.

Dedication

This book is dedicated to my dear mum. You were my biggest cheerleader. You gave me the courage to be myself, to know I was good enough and to take the steps to get my message out into this world. Your unconditional love and support knew no bounds. You are, and forever will be my inspiration, my power and my hero.

Your life shines on in me. I know that you're looking down from your heavenly resting place with pride as people read my words. Your spirit glows within me as I walk through life without you, but also closely by your side. Thank you for giving me the strength to know that I am worth it, and I deserve happiness, love and peace.

I will forever "Keep On Keeping On" and live in your memory until we meet again. I love you.

Acknowledgements

I'd like to thank all the team at Inspired by Publishing, especially Chloë Bisson and Angela Haynes-Ranger.

Thank you for your support and advice in getting this book "out there" for the world to see. Thank you for believing in this project and making it possible. I will be forever grateful.

And finally, to my dear boys.

You are and have always been my "Why"!

Together, we are a formidable team. My love for you overflows each day. Thank you for supporting all my crazy dreams. Being your Mum is the best job in the world, and this book is in honour of you both. Without you, nothing would have been possible. Thank you for saving me many times over, even though you didn't realise you were doing this. Thank you for always being on my side, and for giving me the most precious life worth living and worth loving.

Now and always you have been and will always be the greatest loves of my life.

Contents

Introduction	1
Chapter 1 - How to Recover From Hitting Rock Bottom	9
Chapter 2 - How to Let Go and Start to Move On	31
Chapter 3 - Surviving the Early Days of Single Parenting	39
Chapter 4 - Give Yourself a Break	49
Chapter 5 - Superhero Single Mums	67
Chapter 6 - All Things Legal: The Beginning	87
Chapter 7 - All Things Legal: Final Stages of Court	115
Chapter 8 - Surviving Access	141
Chapter 9 - Getting On With Life: Special Occasions	165
Chapter 10 - Getting On With Life: The Day to Day	189
Chapter 11 - The World of Dating	211
Chapter 12 - I'll Take Care of Me for You, If You Take Care of You for Me	227
Chapter 13 - The New Beginning	255
Conclusion	281
References	285

Introduction

"Women are like tea bags, it's not until you put them in hot water that you realise how strong they are."
– Eleanor Roosevelt

Nobody wants to read a boring book about divorce, right?

And why would you want to spend more time thinking about your divorce by reading about it?

When I started researching other available books about divorce, I was horrified that the ones I chose to read were, quite frankly, dull and uninspiring. To this day, I've not actually finished any of them.

That said, this book wasn't written to be published. When I first started writing, I wanted to capture the details of my divorce, and my thoughts and feelings as time went by. What I discovered through my journey many years later is that I could have reached a better place far sooner than I did.

My divorce years were so traumatic that I realised I could help other people navigate the murky waters of divorce and do some good in this world. I could turn my negative into a positive force for women who are going or will go through the same thing. In truth, I spent little time working on myself throughout my divorce. I was so consumed by what was happening in my life, that I missed the one key element that would help me get through it all in a much easier way.

This is one of the main reasons I want you to read my book: No matter what stage you're at, I can help you avoid the big mistakes I made.

After my divorce was complete, I had a monumental task of trying to recover from years of trauma, stress and depression. I don't want this for you and for women around the world.

By focusing on the guidance in this book, I aim to help you find your freedom and start enjoying your new future a lot sooner than you probably believe is possible.

I started to think about getting my message out to the world. Once I'd documented my divorce, I continued documenting how I recovered from it and how I found myself again. I'm not going to lie, this took many years. I needed to do a great deal of work on myself. Over time, the work I did on myself and finding my future transformed my outlook. My key passion and drive became about how I could help women across the globe move on and find their beautiful future post-divorce.

Are you happy? Do you feel stuck? Do you feel trapped in a marriage? Do you feel a great sense of duty to stay in an unhappy marriage or relationship? Do you feel an intense obligation to keep your family together, no matter how hard it gets for you? Do you feel guilty when you even consider breaking up your family home? Maybe your divorce – the abrupt realisation that you are no longer loved, respected, honoured and wanted by your partner – came as a total shock to you.

The pre-, during and post-divorce years bring about many personal challenges and an immense and varied set of negative emotions. This plethora of feelings challenges your whole being, your thinking, your outlook in life and the way you view the world around you. Also, it challenges the way you view yourself. If you feel lost, depressed, anxious, lonely, frightened or desperate, the good news is that this is absolutely normal. You are living in your new normal, and it can feel like an enormous uphill struggle to put the broken pieces of your life back together.

I talk about the divorce years like an express train: You don't know where you're going, you don't know how long it's going to take and you can't get off the blooming train until the end of the track. I have no magic wand for this period, but I can provide you with the tools to help the journey feel less painful, less destructive, less scary and less out of control.

I felt it was important to share my personal stories throughout this book so that you, the reader, can realise it's OK. What you're going through is a shared experience with women around the world. And you have the strength to get to the end of the line just like I did. Using the strategies in this book will ease the pressure and hopefully, maybe, if you're lucky, help you resolve your divorce much more quickly than I did.

And post-divorce? Well, this is the most significant time for you to reconnect with the person you were before all the hurt and despair. I didn't recognise myself once the legalities of divorce were concluded. It took many years to find my self-worth and my confidence. Do you want to find yourself again after divorce? Get on this journey of self-discovery with me and I will help you find a life you could only have dreamt of in your marriage.

You will discover that divorce is an amazing gift of a new life, happiness, freedom and peace.

And let's not forget that pre-, during and post-divorce you will spend some, or maybe many years as a single mum.

Does the enormous pressure of being a single parent fill you with dread and fear? Do you lie awake at night wondering how you're going to cope, emotionally, financially, and mentally?

Raising children challenges every part of our being; raising children while you're breaking inside is like climbing Mount Everest in ballet shoes. I'm here to help you with this, to find your strength as a single parent and discover the bonus and beauty of being a single mum. It's imperative that you look after yourself as number one because you can't look after your children if you don't look after yourself.

You must put yourself first. When you do this work, your parenting work will become joyful and provide you with a great sense of empowerment as a woman and mother.

So, start your pre-, during or post-divorce recovery today and let's create a beautiful life together. I'm not going to tell you it's all going to be easy. But I will tell you it's going to be worth it. You are worth it. Your children are worth it. There is a heavenly life waiting for you at the other end of this book. Go find your power and your magnificent future, because it is waiting for you to receive it.

Do I Really Hate Men?

An interesting question, and one I have asked myself many times over the last few years.

This is not an "I hate men" book, and neither is it just an account of my divorce and the many awful events leading up to and during the process. There are still some things I would not want my children to read and are best discussed with close friends and counsellors.

This book is a candid account of my thoughts, feelings and opinions based on my reality. I don't expect you to agree with me, and I wouldn't want that. Everyone has their own experiences that form their thinking. However, I know that many of my findings and beliefs are shared with my ever-expanding community of superhero single mums.

There you have it, those two little words: "single mum." A club you join when you find yourself alone with your children. You connect instantly with a group of women who suffer the stigma of those two little words. People have low opinions of single mums with multiple children to numerous fathers, dragging up their long-suffering and deprived children on benefits scrounged from the state. They smoke heavily, drink heavily, maybe take drugs and have various sordid sex romps followed by countless introductions of temporary fathers to their children. I'm incensed writing these words, but regrettably many people (men and women) share all or some of these views.

The truth is, many single mums are in fact "superwomen" in the true definition of the word. They are Mum and Dad, they do bring home the bacon, they wipe bums and tears, they tenderly hug their children in times of need, they go to bed and cry in loneliness and sometimes exhaustion, they fix a broken toilet, they nurse their children when sick, they play football in the park, they watch children's TV endlessly, they pack the school bag, they go to the Christmas school play alone, they pay the bills, they work from dawn till bedtime. Get the picture?

When a relationship ends, not only do you find yourself at the start of the uncertainty of divorce, which is just about one of the most stressful periods of your life, but you also are catapulted into the confusing, exhausting and financially difficult status of being a single mum. So, when you're at your lowest point, you must step up your game and be everything to your children. When you're suffering your most punishing and heart-breaking struggles in life, you must help your children cope with their own struggles, as they go through these with their still-developing and fragile emotions. How is this possible? How overwhelmingly unendurable does this seem?

It is possible because it has to be possible. Again, divorce is like an express train that you can't get off. Eventually, the line will cease, and it will be over. No one knows how long this will take for you and when this journey will be ancient history. But believe me, one day it will be done. For me, it took almost six years, and I still suffered in different ways after my divorce was finalised. In truth, I think that experiencing divorce will always be with you and may haunt you in some ways, even long after it's over.

What you must do in these times is to move forward to your newfound good place? If you don't do this, you will let your divorce forever be a part of your future. Endeavour to keep 99% of it in your past. It was, for me, one hard and bumpy journey with some epic lows.

But scattered along the way, there was hope and a glimmer of happiness; a newfound strength and an overwhelming empowerment; and best of all, the closeness I developed with my children.

I hope this book gives you something that will either help you begin this journey or support you to get on the track towards a brighter future and freedom. I hope you can use this book to guide you onto a path of self-awareness and discovery and to help you live the life you deserve to live. There is life after divorce, and finding your path again and connecting with the person you were, before all the sadness and anger, is imperative to a happy future.

Before you continue, I need you to know that I don't hate men! It's important that you know there are many great men out there: fantastic fathers and even single dads trying hard to do a good job.

While I know little about the struggles of single fathers, I presume there are numerous common issues we share with these amazing men, who strive to do the right thing by their children.

Sadly, I must also admit that not all mums are fantastic mums. If you feel that this is you, I hope you find new ways to improve your personal journey through reading this book.

Chapter 1
How to Recover From Hitting Rock Bottom

"You were given this life because you are strong enough to live it."
— Ain Eineziz

I can't get off this train and it's never ending.

It's the train called divorce, by the way. It's on an immensely long track, and at times it seems like there is no end. It consumes every part of your life and your being.

It's there in the morning when you wake up. Yes, you have moments when you can forget, usually during the day when you're working or with your children. But rest assured, when you lay your head on the pillow, the shadows of divorce surround you again.

It becomes something that lives with you in the worst possible way, like a tenant you can't evict. Like a large boulder that you must carry around on your back. It's heavy, it's prickly, it's like a bad smell that follows you. It's a rain cloud where the sun doesn't shine.

Somehow you must learn to live with this; you must. You must learn to function in your daily life with this elephant in the room. An angry violent elephant that lingers in your aura. And somehow you learn to just get on with things. Thinking that it will shortly be over, that things can't get any worse. This must be the low point; I can grow from here. Only to realise that it does get worse, in ways you can't imagine. And you learn to deal with that too. Because you must. You have no choice. You can't make it stop.

That feeling of being completely unable to make the train stop is quite horrific.

As each new year dawns, I would thank God that the previous year was over. This is the year when things will get better. It can't possibly be as bad as the last one? I would convince myself to think, "This is going to be my year." A year when the train stopped. When the sun shone again. When I could wake in the morning and plan my life instead of what I would say in a courtroom. A year when I would close my eyes at night and, with a smile on my face, truly madly deeply realise, that I was, in fact, happy.

This farce went on year after year, until I could no longer be positive. I just hoped for a year that was marginally better. I had no expectations of a brighter future. Life became hopeless. Most of the time I lived a lie, to the people around me and to my children. I didn't know the abyss I was sinking into. I put my face on each day, I could have won an Oscar for pretending that I was coping. I even fooled myself at times.

When you live like this day after day, something eventually must break. You are not made of titanium and there is only so much the human spirit can take before it cracks. Before it explodes. Before you find yourself in a place that is incomprehensible.

Hitting Rock Bottom

I am a person who is organised and structured. I like to plan and I also value security. I know that makes me sound boring, but it's not boring. I just don't like to live life on the edge. I like to feel stable and comfortable with what's going on. That doesn't mean I can't be spontaneous, I just like to feel secure. I think this is why I found it more difficult than most people to live with every part of my life in total turmoil, lacking financial security or having no confidence in my future. I had always had quite an independent spirit, but insecurity didn't sit well with me.

Initially, I felt I could deal with most things that would come to test me. And almost daily there were challenges – whether it was about access for the children, money, solicitors, or whatever. It was a constant onslaught of unsettlement. I dealt with this by putting all my focus into my children, and the odd bottle of wine. Friends too were a great help, as was my mum. I had many low points since long before the split. Two years of low points and unsettlement, not knowing what to do for the best. I was constantly picking myself up, only to get punched in the stomach again. I was getting more and more depressed as all the hope I had left seemed to be fading into oblivion.

Alone with my thoughts, many times I would daydream of the end of the unsettlement. Until the daydreams stopped, I could no longer see the end. Thoughts turned very dark, as hatred, pure hatred, stirred inside me. My attacker, someone I once loved, now condemning me to misery. At times, I could find no energy to hide my mood from my children. I was just going through the motions with them, and that killed me.

But what could I do? I would have disturbing suicidal thoughts. That could be the end, I had the power to end it in the gravest of ways. Yes, I could end my pain, right now it could be over. Just thinking it could be over made this terrible consideration quite beautiful for a second. That was the only thing I wanted and needed. To end this turmoil and strife.

I feel guilty now thinking about the thoughts I had, but at the time they were very real, very powerful and very tempting. This is why I have always said that it's my children who saved me. I could not have undertaken so much pain just for myself. I had my children, and they were the ONLY thing that kept me keeping on. After I had allowed suicidal thoughts to lay in my head for a short time, I would then happily dismiss them because of my boys. It just wasn't an option; how could I leave my boys? That certainly wasn't the answer. I was doing this for them, for us, for our future. I would endure more, I could endure more, I had to. I could not take my life away and leave my boys in such distress. They would never get over their mother committing suicide.

So, in these depressing moments of weakness, wanting to end it all, my saviours came to gently caress my thoughts back to some form of normality. My boys, without whom I know I certainly wouldn't be here. Time and time again, the depressive thoughts came; and every time the love of my children saved me from myself.

So, was that me hitting rock bottom? Unfortunately, it wasn't. What happened next shook my world and I knew that I needed help. In desperation, I had been to see yet another solicitor for a second opinion, as my world was in complete turmoil. Nobody seemed able to help me, everyone told me I was entitled to what I thought I was, but it seemed impossible to get there. I was being battered daily with words, emails, statements, and letters. Pure vicious lies on innocent white sheets of paper. My job was at risk; nothing was going well. Each day was even more of a struggle than usual.

It was a warm evening and both boys were in bed, asleep. I was in a bad place. I opened a bottle of wine and drank, and drank, and drank. Wallowing in my blackness, my chamber of torture, my mind wandering back to ending it all. I had started to hate myself, maybe because I felt so weak. I felt I had nothing to give, to the fight, even to my children. I was a mess, maybe everyone would just be a whole lot better off if I did end it. My pain was now so overwhelming that it overpowered the love I have for my children. The pain felt bigger, more important. I had to end my life just to get this torture out of my life. At that moment, I believed it. I started to think about what would happen to the boys when I was gone. Planning in my head, where they would go, and how they would live. I remember thinking that they would be OK, they would be looked after and at last I would not have to feel anything anymore.

I write these words with tears in my eyes, as it is truly unbelievable I had let my pain overtake the love I have for my boys. I thought it would be OK to kill myself and ending my pain was more important than the pain I would inflict on them if I had carried out this tragic act. That was my rock bottom.

I don't know what it was that snapped me out of this thinking. I just remember having a lightbulb moment. OMG! Am I really sitting here thinking these thoughts? My children had always saved me from thinking it was an option. Now I *was* considering the option. That's how bad it had gotten. Thank God, I stopped. Something inside me must have jolted me back to reality. At that moment, I knew I needed help. I knew this was serious, that I could not risk going to that place again. My children needed me.

The next morning, I went to see my doctor. I was now accustomed to crying in doctor's surgeries. I'd done this many times throughout my life during difficult periods. However, this time was different. For at least five minutes I could speak no words. In my surgery, you never seemed to see the same doctor twice, and he was a gentleman I had not seen before. He showed me so much compassion that day. He kept passing me tissues, constantly as my eyes flooded and my nose ran. Eventually, I told him about my troubles and the events of the previous night. It felt so good just to tell someone about how I felt. I wasn't acting, this was me raw, with all my cards on the table.

He gave me a month off work and sent me for urgent counselling sessions. He spent time with me, talking and building me up again. Helping me to feel stronger and to slowly realise that with help, there was light at the end of the tunnel. He urged me not to think about anything but just to try to be good to myself. He handed me some information and details of websites to get extra support before I left. There were many disgruntled people in the waiting room as I walked out, my head bowed down to disguise my dishevelled face.

Being off work and having some time to relax and just BE, was just what the doctor ordered. Literally. Yes, I felt numb; yes, I felt vulnerable; and yes, I felt concerned. But I also felt a small glimmer of hope. I knew that the most important thing for me in my life now was to do everything in my power to bring this whole affair to an end. That was more important than any financial settlement, more important than getting what was fair. It was everything. My focus became about not going back to that desperate place.

That was why on our next day in court, I decided it was not worth the fight. Through all the lies and deceit, the outcome would be irrelevant if I were no longer here. I decided I was done, to walk away from the fight. Yes, I could have taken things further for a much more significant financial outcome, but that outcome meant nothing if I didn't have my life. I needed my life, my children needed me to live.

How to Deal With the Bitterness

Bitterness is something that slowly eats away at you. You have no option but to control and manage it. Yes, allow yourself to be bitter at times but realise this: Bitterness is ugly, and you didn't do all of this to become an old, bitter and lonely woman. Knowing when to walk away is wisdom. Being able to walk away is courage. Walking away with your head held high is dignity. No matter what you continue to endure, hold your head up and take the high road.

Yes, you're a single mum but you're not showing your children an unhappy marriage. You've escaped that and that's powerful. Learn to put a smile on your face even when you're breaking inside.

I often retreated into myself in these moments of despair and bitterness. Tried to hide away from the world. Faded away from friends and wallowed. But not in front of my children, at times the only energy I had was to shelter my children from my intense pain. I had nothing to spare. So, if that's all you can do at any stage, do that. You must protect your children from the bitterness inside you. Your body image and self-esteem will probably be at an all-time low, you may have jumped off your social circle. If you feel you can do nothing positive, then just know that it will pass. Because all things pass. In time.

Including your bitterness.

Everyone Is OK Now, Except Me!

I felt dead inside, I had a deep void of emptiness; how could I possibly feel again? As I lay in the darkness of the night, I felt nothing but desolation. Like a vast sea drifting nowhere, I'm on a never-ending journey to the bottom, where darkness resides and where I linger in these moments for hours amidst the black murky waters of my soul.

How do I venture forward to at least see a flicker of light from above? The storm reigns still on the surface of my being, maybe I don't want to come up for air until I know it's calm, safe and I can survive. Maybe I am too afraid that the storm will forever stir, sometimes just the rain and other times its fury of thunder and lightning… But nonetheless, a constant storm.

You see I'm not supposed to feel like this. For God's sake, I'm a trained life coach. I know the theory, and I've saved myself in the past. Why can't I do it now? It's over – my divorce is OVER.

I know that it is only by working through the negativity and pushing forward into positive energy that I will succeed in having a better, happier, calmer and more contented life.

But I couldn't seem to stir up enough drive to think like this even for more than a minute. That hugely frustrated me. I'm tremendously disappointed in myself. I'm a phoney. Maybe all that positive thinking is just people deceiving themselves.

Deception or not, it's a nicer place to be, to live.

But a blissfully positive state of mind is not where I've lived for a long time. Right now, I'm struggling to see if there is a good place in my future. Am I trying too hard to find it? Am I not trying hard enough?

Here's one for you: Maybe I didn't fully believe it would happen.

Every now and then I come across the principles of the "Laws of Attraction." The "principle" of this is that to realise good things happening in your life you have to first believe it will happen so you can create that reality.

Just by having unconditional belief in yourself and that everything is possible, it will all come together, and you will get your perfect life. Well, I'm sick of practising and failing at the Laws of Attraction. Think it and it will materialise in your life – will it really? It's too simple!

Speakers on this subject would argue that if you don't realise your full potential, it must mean you don't believe in yourself fully. Well, thanks very much for that, I feel a million per cent worse now. I can't even do that right. I'm doomed.

When you're in a truly bad place, listening to positive gurus and enlightened people who seem to live a perfect life is the most depressing, heart-breaking therapy ever. It has the opposite effect; it's supposed to make you feel better and provide direction. But in truth it makes you feel even more of a negative pile of shit than you were before.

When I'm in a good place, I love an inspiring quote. When I'm in a very bad place I want to shout and scream at them and flush them down the toilet.

It took roughly five long years before the main areas of my divorce were dealt with. All the fighting was over, my days in court were in my past, and my boys were both making good progress at building a new relationship with my ex. For the first time in a very long time, it seemed like I was finally in a good place.

Ahhhhh but how could I relax and start truly living my life with this black cloud hanging over me?

Yes, everyone was in a good place, except ME.

I no longer had to pull myself together and fight the long fight, but I found no comfort in this. In fact, without the fight,

I was left with an empty shell. I was a woman who was so far removed from the person I used to be, that I hardly recognised myself.

I knew at this point that it wasn't over and that the final stage in this whole long and ugly journey was the struggle to find myself again. The struggle to build myself back up, to find some positive energy within my being – an energy that had been completely depleted over the past 5 to 10 years.

One of the main reasons I wanted to get my message out to the world through this book and my podcast was to help people not get to the very bad place I found myself in.

Throughout this book and in the following few pages I share some of the thoughts and techniques I've used to build myself up again. It *is* 100% possible to have a divorce that doesn't take you to thoughts of suicide. But now I can help people to get through the pain and suffering.

My experiences have shaped my world, but growing and reaching heights I couldn't have ever imagined before in my whole life is transformative. We all have the power to make both our lives and the lives of our children overwhelmingly good and positive. And the journey continues as we should forever be striving to reach new heights of enlightenment and peace.

Stop Digging a Hole; Build a Ladder Instead

I want to now give you some practical tools that I used to help me focus on the actions I needed to take to move forward. Believe me, if you don't just simply read about this and actually do the exercises, it will make a significant difference in your life. Even if life currently *feels* hopeless. There is *always* hope, but you need to take action. Once you've been doing the smaller things that help you get out of bed and survive, you can then start tackling the bigger things. How do you start to create your future?

Sometimes we need to hit rock bottom as that is such a bad place, it jolts us into sorting ourselves out. There are four key emotions that we experience: Despair, Decide, Desire and Action!

When we are in the Despair state of our lives, we feel immense pain and can't/don't want to continue. Whatever form despair takes, that's your lowest point. This often leads to a Decision: to change, to not continue to live in depression and despair. To decide to act is powerful, which then leads to a Desire to make change happen. Once you light the embers of desire inside you, you can take Action to create a new and happier life.

When I first read about this cycle, I started to delve into my past experiences – when I hit my lowest points and when I travelled the road to action and recovery. Sadly, I recognised that I had experienced this cycle far too many times in my life. Over many years I have learnt to be more adept at sustaining the desire and action phases. This does help prevent you from spiralling out of control, and the deep lows become less frequent.

But guess what? Yes, it takes work, work, work. We can all spiral out of control but recognising when you're starting to do this is powerful. It prevents many more days in bed and nights devoted to a bottle or two of wine. Recognise you're on a downward path and turn it around. If you're in a hole, stop digging. Instead, figure out how to build a ladder.

Find Your Strength and Your Power

Think of a time when you felt like a lion: Nothing could stop you; you were fierce, determined and on top of the world. You're the best version of yourself. How good it feels when you allow your strength and power to manifest.

Maybe you must go all the way back, to a time in your childhood to remember this feeling? Children can live in this strength day after day, and it's beautiful to watch it grow.

Do you remember? That power and strength are still inside you. Once you realise this, you can tap into it when you need it. You can use it to your advantage, you can use it to rebuild if necessary.

Pain, hurt and difficult times can take their toll. You feel weak and brittle. If you endure long periods of this, your body and mind forget the strong powerful lion you once were. But hear this: That lion is only sleeping, ready to be awakened, ready to pounce back into your life to help you to feel alive again. You just need to reconnect with it.

After my divorce, I didn't recognise myself. All I knew was the person I had become. I didn't know who I was anymore. But in my memory bank, I remembered who I had been. That wonderful free spirit, happy, ambitious, loving, present and powerful girl. She was willing to sail the Atlantic Ocean on a whim and jump off a mountain with a hang glider on her back. But who on earth was she? I remembered, but I didn't recognise her at all.

That was me, it *really* was me. I knew I had been that person before, and she was still deep inside me. I knew I had to find her again. Was it easy? No, of course it wasn't.

However, just the epiphany I had that one day of knowing she was still in me was life-changing. Slowly, over time, the Angela of old awakened. Now, once again I like and recognise myself. I don't want to jump off mountains anymore, but that power and strength I used to do those things has returned.

Find your power and your strength. You *can* and *will* get it back.

Take 100% Responsibility for Your Life and Your Results

Events + Response = Outcome

This is a common feature of personal development books and simply conveys the message of the need to act. I know I've said that a lot. However, once you realise that only you can do this, it becomes easier to get on with it. If you don't make a change, things *will* stay the same and you will continue to feel the way you do now.

Don't accept that pain in your life. Turn on the lightbulb in your head.

Don't Just Read This – DO IT!

Get yourself a pen and notebook, something you can keep for a long time and return to when needed. Find yourself a nice comfortable place to sit with no distractions. Breathe. Breathe again. Relax and feel good about devoting your *time* to make positive steps to change *your life*.

Write down the five things you have already accomplished in life that you're proud of. If you can write more, then go ahead. Sometimes this comes easy, but if it's hard, keep thinking. Look back over your life. Search for the positive things that have happened to you and the good things you've achieved.

Now, write down all the things you want to accomplish in the next 10 years. Don't consider if these things seem possible. What you're doing here is connecting to the YOU deep inside. Big things and small things. You may want to get married or get married again! You might want to learn a new language or visit Timbuktu. Whatever it is, this is your list. Keep on going and don't stop until you have at least 50 things on this list. Think back to the dreams and goals you once had. What were they? Would you still like to accomplish them? Write them down, then keep going until you can't think of one more single thing to write.

OK, you're doing great. Don't give up or leave it there. Don't decide to pick this up later, or next week. Do it *now*!

Give each goal a number, either 1, 3, 5 or 10 years. Consider, if you were to do this, how long do you think it's possible to achieve it? Remember, you're not going to do all of this. But putting a timescale around this is a very important part of this process.

Now that you've broken these down, how many do you have in each timeline?

Identify your four most important year-one goals. Why are they the most important to you? Delve into what difference achieving these goals will have on your life. They must be relatively easy goals to achieve as you've categorised them in year one.

Write down why achieving this goal is important. Detail what impact achieving this goal will have on your life and well-being. How important is achieving this goal? If it's not that important then go back to the why? Or pick another goal from your list that is more important.

Now that you've identified four goals that are possible to achieve in the next year and why they are important to you, spend some time brainstorming each goal.

Write a list of all the ACTIONS you can take that will move you closer to achieving this goal. What support do you need? From whom do you need support? What can you do in the next seven days that will help you to progress towards achieving this goal? Do this with each goal and before your eyes you will see an easy simplified plan that will help you create the positive change you're searching for.

Taking time to invest in doing this could be the most instrumental turning point in your life. Don't just read these words. If someone stops you in the street and says, "Give me 30 minutes and I can and will change your life forever, and it's not going to cost you a penny," would you do it? Of course, you would. Why the hell not? I recommend planning 30 minutes every week or every two weeks to work on this little book of awesomeness that you're creating. Each time you do this, come away with actions to do before your next planned time. Slowly moving forward. Slowly making positive change. You will be amazed at the opportunities that can open for you just by simply devoting time to work on *you*.

As you work, week on week or month on month, keep adding and deleting your goals. Your priorities and goals can change and it's important to not beat yourself up if you no longer feel connected to a goal. When I was nineteen, I sailed across the Atlantic Ocean. And since I did that, and for many years afterwards, I had a goal to sail across the Pacific Ocean. Whenever I looked at my goals I would feel less and less inclined to do this but felt as though deleting it from my list would be admitting I had failed. I have not failed, I have just grown and changed. Other things are now more important to me. Remember, there is no right and wrong with this exercise. This is the essence of who you are and your deepest wishes and aspirations. For many people, this is deeply personal. I rarely share this list with anyone, it is for me and me alone and helps me to be positive about my future.

The purpose of this exercise is not to achieve everything on the list, but to keep you moving forward. Indeed, you may achieve a lot if you continue to put the work in. Most importantly you're moving forward and it's imperative that you celebrate every success along the way. You are creating your own destiny and that is awesome. YOU are awesome, unique, brilliant, worthy, and loved.

A final note on this: If you can, try to incorporate some personal development goals into your list. Investing in your personal development is the greatest gift you can give to yourself.

It's Not Pain That Destroys You – It's Guilt

As a mother, father, and parent we can become consumed by guilt. Guilt that we are not good enough. Or that we are not doing enough. Or that we are not a model parent. Or that we don't live up to what we see other parents doing.

We see parents at the school drop off with their seemingly perfect lives and feel we need to do more. As a single parent, you see couples at school, and we feel we have failed our children. Even if we don't believe these things 100% of the time, we may only believe them 2% of the time. Guilt creeps in and takes hold of us. If we look at outside influences, then we will never be a good parent. In fact, what even is a good parent? People parent in many ways and there is no right or wrong, no good or bad, no handbook to explain where you're going wrong or which path to take. We navigate parenting as total novices. And by the time we've worked out what to do and how to react, they grow, and the challenges change. New challenges develop with each couple of years that pass by. So, we are forever trying to figure out the best way to deal with different situations and circumstances.

Here's a tip: Give yourself a break.

No wonder you are stressed, a little bit mad, exhausted, breaking down even with how overwhelming this job of being a parent is. Being a parent is the hardest job you will ever love. I will say that again, it's the hardest job you will ever love. And we do love it. Immensely. But we somehow can default to feelings of guilt many times, especially in the first 18 years. Beyond this we still parent, but in different ways. Hopefully, after 18 years, we've learnt that guilt is a waste of time and of no benefit to anyone – whether to the parent or the child. All we can do as parents is strive to do our very best each day, in the same way that, as human beings, all we can do is strive to be the very best human, every single day. Yes of course you will have moments and days you're not proud of, that have been immensely hard. What we need to do is to wake up the next day and reset. Striving to go again, fail, get back on the horse and carry on.

Guilt can manifest in many ways over our lifetime, and it is the most destructive emotion for us. Every guilty person is his own hangman. Guilt is a destructive and ultimately pointless emotion, an emotion that we bring upon ourselves, in our own minds. Nobody is perfect. In law, a man is guilty if he violates the rights of others, don't violate your own life with feelings of guilt. Learn how to control these feelings and rationalise them. Take time to identify feelings of parental guilt and have a word with yourself. Give yourself a break. You will not get parenting right 100% of the time. Don't beat yourself up when you feel you've made a mistake. Own it, apologise if necessary, and commit to trying to aim to do better but *please don't destroy your mental health with feelings of guilt*.

Everyone Can, But Not Everyone Will

Believe what is possible for you, go to work and make it real. The only impossible journey is the one you never begin. Those are powerful words; they are hugely inspiring. Often, we feel immense passion and drive to create our future, but we still don't take sustained and constant action to make things happen. What in life is more important than working on creating a better life for ourselves and our children? Even as I write these words, I look back at all the times I've procrastinated. Stood still, sometimes for months and even years.

Ask yourself: What kind of person must I become to achieve all I want? It's not what you get that makes you valuable, it's what you become that's valuable. What you become helps you to achieve and what you achieve helps you to become. These are serious questions we need to spend time evaluating. What changes can you make right now to help you become the person you want – or need – to be?

If you're struggling with this, then turn it around. What do you need to *stop* doing to become the person you want to be? Start with the small stuff. I need to stop watching four hours of Netflix every night. I need to stop wasting money on expensive handbags. Take some time to make a list of all the things you want to *stop* doing. Now pick three things you want to *stop* right away. Maybe the easy options are a good place to start. After two weeks re-visit the list and choose another three things you want to *stop* doing. Over time you will produce more time to create the person you want to become. Start now. Don't put off to tomorrow what you can do today. Reading these words is a fantastic start. But start you must.

Chapter 2
How to Let Go and Start to Move On

This is an interesting one. We quite often look to outside influences to improve our lives, our situation, and our future. And I think we do this because it's easier to blame others when things don't go our way. In fact, the sooner you realise that your fate is completely and *only* in your hands, the sooner you realise that *you* and *you* alone have the power to change your universe. Then things become a little easier.

You have more focus when you have nobody to blame. Many times, I accepted my lot and just waited for good things to come: For others to have an impact on my life, and to just get on with life while waiting for a miracle to happen, like winning the lottery or meeting the man of my dreams. And although I have tried to manifest those things, I also needed to realise that my future and my destiny need work. They need my 100% attention, and an awareness that I make my own future with small but consistent steps each day. So, if you feel alone and need a helping hand, look to the hands that are completely in *your* control.

Put your hands to good work each day on *your* future. This can be something as simple as doing a Google search, writing a diary or blog, or researching something you want to materialise in your life. *You* have the hands to help yourself. So why do we not use them? Why do we not use what we already have each day to improve our lives? If I'm being honest, it's because it takes a daily commitment to a goal or a desire, and that takes working through the distractions of life. Every day, new intrusions come up that take us away from our true purpose. It could be work, kids, financial issues, the TV, a night out with friends, or a significant other. We ultimately forget about this daily drive for a better life. Life gets in the way and you spend the next few months surviving and getting nowhere. In my case, it took a few years. In some people's cases, their entire lives.

If you really decide to make a change – and usually this comes after a prolonged period of discomfort that forces you to take action – you need to start by using your own hands each and every day. If you need a helping hand, look at the end of your arms. ☺

It's easy to let our past define our future. Our experiences make up who we are, and explain the scars we have. But on a positive note, they also help us see the world with empathy and understanding. The most difficult experiences of my life have certainly left their mark on me and I work hard every day to *not* let them define me and my future. You see, this "stuff" takes work, we don't just have a thought to let go of our past and it magically goes away. You must live with the awareness and determination to move forward with a different mindset. It sounds easy, but it takes work. It's easy to ride the positive wave of good times, but what defines our true strength and growth is how we then deal with the strains and stresses, the disasters, the hurt, the loneliness, and the despair. Because to live a life expecting these things *not* to happen is truly naïve. What we *can* expect if we continue to grow is to deal with these tribulations a little better than before.

And if we falter once or twice, *do not give up!*

Get back on the road to positivity and growth. An enlightened mind is thankful for hard times. These experiences help us to recognise when someone needs our help. They encourage us to reach out and extend love and compassion for others. They also help us to appreciate the good times: those bright days, when the sun shines the whole day through and you're living your best self.

As for the future? Well, only time will tell. I do know that I have spent many wasted hours worrying about my future. My boys' future. This worry clouds the mind and is exhausting. Sometimes we let it take over our whole being and we live in fear. That's the absolutely worst state to reside in. Living in fear stops the natural flow of life and closes all doors to opportunities. Living with fear manifests more fear and can have devastating effects, sometimes leading to considering if it's worth continuing. I have visited these very dark moments in life on more than just a few occasions. The silver lining in these times is that they can be a momentous turning point. Sometimes we need to hit rock bottom before deciding to act, to better things. In fact, most times we *need* to hit rock bottom to make the changes we must make, for a better life.

Life is like a car on a production line. I'm not the new, shiny and perfectly complete car at the end. I'm just halfway, with quite a few bits missing. Sometimes the machine stops, and I need oil or fixing, a new bit added, or an engineer to get me working again.

What I'm trying to say here is stop trying to be the finished article on your life's journey. We should never be "finished," unless we're standing still (which we quite often are); we should be growing and learning new things. It doesn't have to be ground-breaking; we just need to be improving and blossoming into a better version of ourselves. It's OK to be broken for a while, it's OK to be down for a period of time.

Especially when life throws us a hard lesson or a sour pill to swallow. Recognising that we can't stay broken and damaged is extremely powerful. If all you can do is one positive thing in the day, then just do that and you're moving forward. In life, I have experienced many times when I just couldn't muster the strength to get myself out of bed, for days on end. But when the time is right, get up and take a walk. Get up and read a passage from your favourite book. Get up and out into nature and breathe the fresh air of a new day. Clear a messy draw, tidy your wardrobe, and throw away things in your house you no longer need. These small things help us on the road to recovery, and slowly you can rebuild. You may feel like a rusty old car, but if you start to love that car and work to mend it, life WILL open up for you. You may think everyone around you is doing better than you, but believe me, even a £100,000 supercar can break down. So go forth and create the future you desire. I've always had a concrete belief in fate and destiny. I have had many discussions with people who mock this belief. However, what they don't understand and sometimes fail to comprehend is that just because you believe in fate and destiny doesn't mean you can just sit back and let it all happen. You must think, contemplate options, decide a course of action, and just *do* something – whatever that "something" is that you decide to do is your destiny. You could say, you create your own destiny.

Indeed, you do, however you were destined to. That is just my belief. All I am saying is that we achieve nothing by standing still. Action, no matter how small, is progress. Only you can decide to take action.

The Beginning of the End

I had not been happy for a long time. We had been married seven years and together eight. I had seriously contemplated leaving my husband for two years before I finally plucked up the courage to do it. It's an exceedingly hard decision, and probably one of the most defining decisions of your life: to resolve to break up your family. To decide to put your children through a childhood of a broken marriage. To decide to become a single mum, to decide to go it alone.

These are hefty decisions. The only way I can describe it is that for two years I had decided I couldn't do it. I couldn't do it to my children. But when things got so bad for me, I eventually decided I had no option but to do it – for my own sake, and my children's sake. We were all intensely unhappy. I had always believed that children deserve happy parents. My parents were unhappily married for two and a half decades before they finally separated when I was in my early 20s. Because of this, I knew that children deserved to live with parents who actually wanted to be together, who showed love and affection to each other, and who cared for each other.

I did genuinely try hard to "make it work." I attempted to talk to my husband about some of the issues that made me unhappy. I suggested that we go to counselling in my endeavour to stay together and mend what was broken. Counselling only made things worse for us, unfortunately. He paid lip service when speaking with the therapist, so after what was to be our last session, I finally broke.

I could no longer endure it and I suggested that we needed some time apart. Maybe if he had time without me, he would realise how much he loved and needed me. Maybe with a little time apart, he would realise that he truly madly deeply still loved me? I know it was a romantic and useless hope, but the thought that he actually just didn't give a damn (the way his words and actions made me feel) was just too much to bear. Over the following days, weeks, months, and years, I concluded that he really didn't give a damn, and that he never did. Coming to terms with that is gruelling; moving on from it is even harder. I remember after that final counselling session we returned home, and he started to pack a bag. The children were with a friend and I was due to collect them later that evening. He was just about to leave the house when he turned to me and said, "If I walk out of that door, I am never coming back!"

WOW. I had suggested some time apart, but this was so final. I now know that in these first few weeks, he was 100% certain that I, weak, feeble, and inadequate Angela would come crawling back to him, begging him to take me back. Because he thought I was nothing without him. He thought I would crumble into hopelessness without him. Don't get me wrong, I crumbled many times. But I also dug deep and found the strength to leave the man I vowed to love and honour for the rest of my life. The man I had fallen in love with in that magical first year of being together was now unrecognisable to me.

It was a few years after the split that I discovered the meaning of the word "narcissist" – a person who has an excessive interest in or admiration of themselves. I was reading about divorcing a narcissist and how difficult it was to do. In truth, I'm glad that I didn't know what was before me at that time. The following years that I describe in this book nearly broke me, but it also gave me my life back too.

In her article "Help! I'm Divorcing a Narcissist" on *Psychology Today*, Dr. Karly McBride, Ph.D says:

"If you marry a narcissist and then divorce that person, the narcissist will not forgive and forget. They do not move on easily. They cling to "How could you abandon me or do this to me" and the anger lingers for long periods of time...sometimes years and years. To imagine that one could process an amicable divorce with a narcissist and stay friends and co-parent in a reasonable manner is not realistic with narcissists. They do things like excessively disparaging the other parent and resort to making up unfair and untrue allegations. Their entitlement needs get in the way of fairly dividing property and money and in the end, they do not think of what is best for the child or children. They think about what is best for them! "It is my parenting time!"

Because narcissists do not have the capacity for empathy and emotionally tuning in to the needs of others, the children's emotional needs are not realised. Thriving on constant conflict is the narcissist's way to stay connected and fight for his or her own rights rather than consider what works for the children. In fact, being oblivious to the needs of the children is usually observed."[1]

Why one would marry a narcissist is a no-brainer. They can be charming, enticing, engaging and easily put on a show in the beginning of relationships. They are out there for you to fall in love with. You will only know the reality as you get to know them better over a period of time. But...if you decide to divorce, reach out for some specialised assistance! You and your kids are worth it.

Chapter 3
Surviving the Early Days of Single Parenting

The early days of our divorce are a bit of a haze, if I'm being honest. Looking back, I suppose it's the calm before the storm. And by "storm," I am referring to the time after solicitors get involved and you find yourself in a courtroom.

The first obvious task was to tell the children, which was left for me to do alone. Somehow you find the words and the power to be strong while you're breaking inside. My eldest was 10, he was the worst affected initially, as he was emotionally proficient enough to realise that big changes were ahead. My youngest boy – bless him – was only six, and although he was upset, he couldn't really assimilate what it all meant for him and our family. His struggles would come a few years later.

It was October and my eldest's last year in Primary school. I had just changed my job to accommodate being able to finish at 4pm instead of 5pm. However, all I remember of the early days was the great difficulty of trying to look after the boys *and* hold down a full-time job. My husband had always had a very flexible job, so he did a fair majority of picking the boys up and making tea. Now I had to do all this by myself.

Trying to arrange contact and agree on access arrangements around these restrictions was even more difficult. We tried a few different rotas, and nothing was a great fit. I knew this was never going to be easy. On top of the physical and practical problems, there was the small complication of how we could overcome our difficulties in communicating with each other. It was very strained, and honestly, he tried to make my life as difficult as possible. He refused to pick the kids up from school and let me have them. If he picked them up, they stayed overnight with him. I had to arrange and pay for childcare to fit around his access. Many arguments followed, and I found myself slowly coming to terms with the fact that this man, whom I had been married to, detested me now. He was doing everything he could to make my life as uncomfortable and difficult as possible.

Through all the disagreements and failed access schedules, the single most difficult issue I had to deal with at this time was the time I spent without my children. Whole weekends spent lonely, craving for a kiss and a cuddle from my boys. I wondered how they were, what they were doing, if they missed me and if they were OK. Hours and hours of what was once a busy family life now lay silent. My home was like a monastery, where the love of God had abruptly ceased to live. Without my boys, my home was quiet and lifeless, a shelter for nothing. It was a loveless place of deep loneliness, and I hated it. For the first 12 months, I hardly ventured out. I wallowed in the darkness of my home alone, not wanting to face life without my boys. However, when I did have my boys, the house became a haven of love, comfort, refuge, togetherness and happiness. We were a family, living together, just the three of us, in the house where the four of us had been so unhappy. We had a new sense of freedom and purpose. We were blissfully happy just because we were *not* unhappy living there anymore. Rather than living in fear, the boys ultimately became more relaxed.

I called my ex-husband The Sergeant Major. He believed that you should be able to cure children of being naughty. They didn't get a second chance if they didn't do as he said the first time. He became extremely angry. I was always there to calm the situation down; however, now we didn't have to live under that fear. We all felt the freedom of being able to fully relax at home, and we loved it.

What Do I Do Now?

Another one of the hardest things to overcome is how you attempt to deal with all the changes in your life. Because just about *everything* changes. You have to learn how to hold down a job, deal with childcare, do *all* the cooking and shopping, remember which night to put the bins out, be strong for your children, and take them out at weekends while hiding the fact that you're breaking down inside, paying the bills, and deciding on a solicitor (more on that one later). The list is endless, and you need to be prepared for this and try to adopt a "one thing at a time" approach for most things. I know I've just mentioned hiding your feelings from your children. And *yes*, we absolutely have to do this, although there are times when it is good for your children to see the more fragile side of you. For them to see that you find all of this hard too.

You *must* talk about your feelings with your children so that they can learn from this and *share their feelings with you*.

So it's OK to be vulnerable sometimes in front of them. It really does help both them *and* you. Just make sure your feelings of strength and love supersede your vulnerability or they will start to feel abundantly brittle, delicate and insecure. And you really don't want that for them. Many people fall into this trap, and it's so tempting and easy to do. However, you must not speak badly about the father of your child in front of them, no matter how awful he is to you or how much you loathe him at that moment. Do not share your negative feelings about him with your children. He could be the worst father in the world, but bite your lip and find someone else to vent your anger to.

Be the Best Parent You Can Be

Parenthood is, without a doubt, the hardest job you will ever love. Of course, we all want to be the best parent we can be; however, navigating the tidal wave of parenthood can be overwhelming at times. Especially if you are a single parent. I hate when people refer to single parents as having "broken homes." It's not. Do you know what is a broken home? Having a house full of people who shouldn't be together and letting that toxic energy bleed into their kids.

That is a broken home.

I remember when I was first on my own with my two boys. The sense of freedom was unbelievable. We were all now totally relaxed in our home. It was like a massive cloud had been lifted. Overnight there was no longer tension. I suppose I didn't realise just how much anxiety we were living with until it was just me and my boys. I call this the "honeymoon period" of a breakup. Not everyone will experience this, but if you have been living in a very restricted and controlled way, the liberation is blissful. It would have been wonderful to continue living in this manner, but the dark, practical side of divorce slowly creeps in, and somehow you must manage that. You must be strong and be a parent during absolute turmoil. And when you break, you must heal, because your children don't deserve the broken version of you. Otherwise, what was it all for? How you survive and how quickly you get back on track will have an everlasting effect on your children. Your children don't need you to save them, they need to watch you save yourself.

I'll Take Care of Me for You, If You Take Care of You for Me

The greatest gift you can give your children is the best version of you.

We become so wrapped up in being a parent, that we forget to look after ourselves. Nothing else matters apart from the well-being and happiness of our children, right? And I agree with this to a point. Our greatest source of happiness is our children. But they need to see you living and breathing and striving to be better – the best version of yourself. Everything they have learnt about life so far has come from you; both good *and* the bad. A common mistake we make with older children is we forget they are still learning about life, from *us*! So be kind to yourself, love yourself and give yourself a break. Only by giving to yourself can you truly give to your children. Think of the safety briefing when you're on an aeroplane. When they explain the procedure to put a life mask on that will magically drop from the ceiling, they advise you to fix your own mask first. Only then should you attend to your children or babies. Make sure you can breathe and function so you can help your children to do the same.

Wow. That's so powerful, isn't it? Take this thought process with you in life.

Talk About What's Going On in Your Head and Your Heart

We've already discussed the need to talk to your children, share your thoughts and bring to life your past stories. I also believe that it's important to be honest with your children. Let them know what you're doing, what you're thinking and what major things affect family life. Allow yourself to be vulnerable with your children as they get older. Be honest when you're feeling down; talk about your feelings. If you never talk about your feelings how can they learn to talk about theirs? I don't mean to share the negatives or the worries and stresses of life. But tell them what you're thinking of doing, and what options you may be considering. Don't keep secrets about things that may also affect your children. Share with them your strategies to overcome unexpected bumps in the road. You're preparing them for life and how they can handle these issues as adults. With younger children, it's important to listen so that they feel heard. You may know that they are worrying about nothing, and you may have significant things going on in your life that are more important. However, your children's feelings need to be heard.

One friend of mine very rarely shared anything with her son. At times, I witness him finding out significant things from friends or by listening to phone conversations. This breeds uncertainty and mistrust. How can you expect your children to open up to you and share what's going on in their lives if you can't do the same? This encourages them to come to you for advice later in life, in an environment of no judgement. Remember, even as teenagers they are still learning about life. How you interact with them as teenagers gives them life skills for adulthood. Don't be too hard, don't be too strong. If they need you, make sure you listen with conviction. Stop what you're doing, give them your time without distractions.

Communication is *everything* with younger and especially older children. Show them how to communicate by communicating *with* them. Be open, be honest. Show them your power and sprinkle discipline with love. They must always know and feel your love for them. You can still love them but hate what's happening with them. This is especially true when dealing with bad behaviour and teenage tantrums. These stages usually pass with time, but it can be extremely difficult to communicate when there is friction.

Pick your battles and pick your time to talk. I find that when communication is an issue, a great time to talk is when you're all in the car. There is nowhere for them to escape. Teenagers can lock themselves in their bedrooms for days on end, but catch them in the car and there is nowhere to hide! Bedtime is the best time to get younger children to open up. They are usually relaxed and feel safe in the comfort of their bed. Encourage them to talk about their day. Give them the simple recognition and support that they need. Tell them how loved and valued they are. I remember, for at least six months before my youngest was due to do his first exams at school, he would despair every night about his ability to get through it. He worried for six whole months – bless him – at the tender age of nine years. Could I stop him from worrying? No. But I could help him to deal with this, and be a vehicle for these worries to surface and not eat away inside him. Yes, it could be exhausting and very repetitive at times, as each night the same concerns would surface, and I used mainly the same words to comfort him. It takes time for the penny to drop, to work through these worries and woes in a child's head. Be patient and your time, effort, care and love will be the healing power and energy they need.

If we could prevent our children from suffering, we would, right? But we can't, they must grow themselves as we do. This growth and pushing of their boundaries mean they must face fears and overcome obstacles. Help them to do this by listening and communicating. Don't just read a story as quickly as you can at bedtime. Use this time to hold them dearly in your hands and guide them through the stumbling blocks of life.

If the Parents Are OK, the Kids Are OK – Not 100% But Mostly

Happy parents actually do equal happy children – not all the time but a fair amount of the time. Therefore, you *must* look after yourself. This is not selfish in any way but an essential part of parenting. Of course, if you always put yourself first then you're totally missing the point here. The worst thing to imagine is a child constantly having to worry about their parent. We tend to think of these instances as extremes, but your children may be concerned about you for little or no reason. If you're not looking out for yourself, loving yourself and making yourself happy, try turning this around so they can see the change. Let them be witnesses to you following your passions and enjoying life.

I created a list of all the things I like to do, and I would go to this list when I had some spare time for myself. I love going to the cinema, walking in beautiful places, watching the sea and breathing the sea air. I love going to a coffee shop and just sitting, watching the world go by. Use your time wisely when you don't have your children around, and share with them what you have been doing, your version of self-care. Too often, parents hide their emotions from their children – both the good and the bad. You're not a robot, so show them how you're feeling. Let them ride the waves of happiness and a little sadness with you, together. It's only by sharing your strategies for pain and suffering that they build their own strategies for dealing with this thing called life. Of course, you can't show them your deep depression, months of sadness and mental health issues. That's not what I'm saying. If you need help to deal with your pain, then you must get this help urgently before your children are affected by it. The trauma a child feels in extreme situations where they feel fearful for their parents can affect them their whole lives and their ability to parent in years to come.

So, make time for *you*.

Your children *need* you to do this and to take good care of yourself. Remember the safety information when you board a flight? Make sure you put your own oxygen mask on or before you help children to do the same. It's powerful stuff. Take care of yourself as that enables you to care for your little ones and everyone around you.

Chapter 4
Give Yourself a Break

If you only take away one piece of parenting advice, then I urge you to make it this:

Be present!

Yes, it's that simple. Children want and crave our time. Younger children just want us to get on the floor and play with them, their cars, trains, dolls, and building blocks. It's that simple.

Don't just get up on weekends and watch TV while they play. Play with them. Make up games together, and create dens out of blankets and old sheets. Time invested in these small things is so important to your relationship with your children, and how they value you.

I'm not saying you need to be Super Mum or Super Dad, but so many parents don't get one-on-one time with their children like this. Or maybe they do, but they don't use the time they have effectively. I've observed parents at the park constantly on their phones while their children play. It breaks my heart. Especially when you see the child shouting over, "Look at me, Mummy!"

All your children want is for you to focus on them more than just occasionally. Get off the phone, stop scrolling through your social media and be present with your children.

How often do you see parents in a restaurant with their children on tablets or devices? Parents bring these objects so that the children can be distracted. So that they can have an "adult conversation" or not need to manage bad behaviours.

How about this: Why not talk to your children? Engage with them, ask them how they are. Have fun together.

Single Parenthood "Forces" You to Be Present

In my view, this is one of the wonderful advantages of being a single parent. You don't have another adult to converse with, so you become skilled and find great happiness in the presence of just your precious children. As they become older, the conversations you can have while in a restaurant turn into deep and meaningful conversations, sharing stories and family tales.

Writing this takes me back to a holiday in Cape Verde with my boys. We booked into a very lovely five-star Chinese restaurant to celebrate my eldest son's birthday. We were one of the first to arrive and the last to leave. We were having so much fun. I was sharing stories about my life in my late teenage years and early twenties. They were fascinated and asked so many questions. We laughed and they saw a side of Mum they didn't know was there.

In fact, there is very little my boys don't know about my life. They have a solid picture of my childhood, what I've done, jobs I've had and what I've learnt along the way. I can't stress this enough: Take time to be present and share your life with your children.

I urge you now to stop reading for a short while to reflect on your own situation. What changes do you need to make in your life? How can you inject more quality family time into your week or month?

Write a list in your journal of all the things you might want to stop, start or continue doing. Now look at this list and commit to two or three of these things. Choose the easy ones first; start small and work yourself up to the bigger changes you want to make. Keep this list close and revisit it often. Or take 30 minutes each week to review how you can make the next week better than the last.

You can't get these early years back. They go so fast, but you don't quite see this when your children are young. You can feel as though you've got years and years of being a parent to small children. But in the whole scheme of things, once they branch out on their own, you will only have memories of this time. Today is when you make these memories, not tomorrow. Don't wait; do it now.

Work on not only being with them, but also being present with them, giving your children more of your attention. I advise you to consciously spend the next few days looking for the activities you do alongside having your children around. When you're in the car or on the school run. Are you also talking on the phone? On weekends, how much valuable one-on-one time do you devote to your children? Do you actively watch the TV with them, laugh at the same funny stories, or are you sat beside your little ones looking at the next big thing on Instagram?

When my two were still very young, I had a very stressful and demanding job. But my husband didn't. He would often skive off work and go home for an afternoon snooze. It always amazed me how he got away with this when I hardly had time in my day for a break, and most days ended still with a mountain of emails to attend to. Despite this unbalance, my ex-husband and I would take turns to get up with the boys on weekends. They were early risers, and never really slept past 6am, even after a late bedtime.

This worked well; however, there was one significant difference. I would get up and we would go downstairs and put children's programmes on the TV and get out numerous toys to play with. When it was Dad's turn, he would watch what *he* wanted to on TV. Not a stuffed puppet or animated dog in sight. He would either watch football intently or documentaries about World War 2. If the boys asked if they could watch a cartoon, it was an outright no. So of course they stopped asking. He never gave his time to them; he was in the room but was hardly ever present. I found this very upsetting and often questioned him about it. But it fell on deaf ears.

Now I'm not saying I was a perfect Mum; far from it. Yes, there were some weekend mornings when I was on my laptop catching up on emails from the previous day. I'm not proud of that, but I did it so I could then enjoy the rest of the weekend with no distractions from work.

A few years later I worked hard towards doing very little work at home. Or when I did, it was when the boys were still sleeping. When I became a single mum even later, I felt a great responsibility that my boys only had me to help them navigate the pain of their parent's separation. I did that by throwing every inch of myself into being the best parent I could be.

Was I perfect? Absolutely not, but striving for this each day is a gift you give your children for life. Beating yourself up has no value; however, being mindful and trying to do your best to be present as much as you can is transformational.

Just think about the distractions of life that, over time, build a void between you and what's important in your life. You can't go back and rewrite the last 18 years of parenting. Make sure your children feel loved, valued and important. The way you do this is by giving them *your uninterrupted time.*

Be Kind, Be Honest, Be Open

I know this isn't exactly ground-breaking advice, is it?

But do you stick to this rule in every aspect of your life? In good times and in bad? So many times, I have had thoughts of mischief, of getting my "own back" on people who have wronged me. I can honestly say that no matter how tempting, I have always listened to the voice inside me telling me when something is wrong. And I've lived by that wholeheartedly.

Even today, when I walk past my ex's shiny new sports car, thoughts of inflicting a little scratch on the paintwork ping into my mind. Or even a big, mother-of-all-scratches from front to back! Oh, how lovely to think of the look on his face when his source of pride and joy has been disfigured. He deserves no less when you look at the pain he has inflicted on me over the past 15 years.

Yes, one can almost justify criminal damage in these moments, can't we?

I have a saying now about this very thing. "Well boys, at least I know I'm going to heaven!" Call it a moral compass, that sense of right or wrong. No matter how much someone has wronged you, they will get their retribution in the end. I want no part in stooping to their level just to gain five minutes of gratification from it.

I have been wronged by so many people in life. I have lost thousands of pounds to the cruel actions of people who once claimed to love me. By extended family members whose greed stole my inheritance. Money really does bring out the worst in people, doesn't it?

Of course, I am no angel. But no matter how strong the urge to hit back, respond, retaliate, reciprocate…just don't do it. You will feel much better in the long term. In the short term, it feels good to hurt someone who has deeply hurt you. But let it go. Be kind, be honest, be open. *That* feels good.

Losing and Gaining Friends

From that sombre day that my ex-husband walked out of the house, I have had absolutely no contact with any of his family or friends. Friends, who had become my friends over seven or eight years, just disappeared off the face of the earth.

No phone call to ask how I was. Only one friend of my ex sent me a short text message saying how sorry he was. To this day, I have not had a conversation with any of his family, not even his mum. I was completely disowned by everyone. Over time I came to ascertain that many lies had been told concerning our split. Eventually, one also comes to realise that you have no control over what other people do and say about you and your situation.

If it made him feel better to tell his friends I was having an affair, then what could I do? I was in a war of words with my ex daily, and I didn't want to engage in war with his family and friends too. So, I stayed quiet and just did what I needed to do for my boys and for myself.

It's important to point out here that the old saying of finding out who your real friends are in times of adversity is also very true. You need some good friends in your life, and even if you only have one or two close friends, they can be instrumental in helping you through the darker days of divorce.

Nonetheless, you will find that some friends don't care for your new "single" label, and they especially want you to stay away from their husbands. I mean, just because you're going through a divorce doesn't mean you want to steal someone's spouse. In fact, in my experience, it probably makes you want to run a mile in the opposite direction – away from men altogether.

You will find that as you go through life as someone "getting a divorce," you enter a very special club: The Divorce Club. It's very common and you will meet and have a deeper understanding of anyone who has gone through or is going through a divorce. It's in this space that I made one particularly good friend, a friend for life. She is the only person I have met who has had a more difficult divorce than myself; a very different voyage than mine, but still a harrowing journey.

You will also learn that everyone you meet has had the "worst divorce ever." This is because it's such a personal and harrowing experience. How could anyone go through more than you've endured? Every divorced man I have met was "taken to the cleaners by his ex-wife." Who knows and who am I to judge? All I know is many people lose a great deal of money. I know I did. And we lose so much more than that. Money can be replaced with hard work, determination and dedication. Emotions and feelings are more difficult to repair and replace.

Some people tell you their "divorce story" and you think, "Wow, you had it easy compared to me." Nevertheless, your journey is your journey, and just because others have had it "easy" doesn't mean it was not extremely arduous for them to deal with. You will find that your friends in The Divorce Club are helpful confidants, as they *do* completely understand you. When you say you can comprehend a crime of passion, they don't judge you. They know that the feelings you go through are extreme and real. So, go forth and find your new friends and embrace their stories. You can help each other tremendously.

One or two honest and faithful friends – you know the ones you can ring up at 3am and who will be there for you no matter what – will make this experience a whole lot easier. And they will usually supply a good amount of wine at the same time.

I remember one awful evening during the first year. I'd had a very burdensome and gruelling day with my ex. After I'd put the children to bed, I sat on the sofa and sobbed. I didn't have one drop of wine in the house, and boy, did I need a drink.

Now, I'm not a lover of airing your dirty laundry on Facebook and I certainly didn't give an account of my divorce or my anger and misery. However that night, I posted a comment about how there is never any wine in the house when you really need it. About ten minutes later the doorbell rang. It was my next-door neighbour with a large bottle of full-bodied glorious red wine in her hand. She passed it to me and softly said, "Here, I think you need this tonight." I couldn't get any words out, she knew I was just a bag of shambles and I was not in a place where I could even talk. As she turned away, she said that she was there if I needed anything.

Wow. I've never forgotten that one gesture. It meant so much to me in that moment. Later that week, I bought her favourite bottle of wine and re-paid the favour, along with a thank you note for being there in my hour of need.

Wine, Wine, and More Wine

Unless you are teetotal before this journey, you need to be prepared to drink way more alcohol than you've ever drunk before.

Almost everyone I have spoken to about divorce has divulged that wine got them through on more than one occasion. Sometimes, it just takes the edge off, and sometimes we drink into a stupor so we can forget our unpleasantness – for a short time at least.

I'm certainly not proud of the amount of alcohol I drank over the numerous years of my divorce, but it helped me through. I have, however, on more than one occasion, had to reel myself in, as it would have been so effortless and tempting to drink every night, to a point where I could forget. That's when it gets dangerous and you're verging on alcoholism, so be careful.

A good friend and a bottle of wine can help ease many painful situations, and my friends were awesome on many occasions. But I confess to frequent nights alone with my bottle, drinking in misery, in loneliness, in despair, in pure panic for my future, in anger, in exasperation, in trepidation, in fear, in anxiety, in depression, in exhaustion, into bed. Not really feeling better, but feeling a little less pain…until tomorrow.

So, whatever your chosen drink, be it wine, beer, gin, or vodka, be wary; but also don't beat yourself up about your drinking. If it helps, then that's a good thing. Even better is if you can find another outlet for stress relief, like the gym, running, writing or white-water rafting. Whatever helps you through…Hiccup!

Negative Is Normal; Learn How To Manage It

Did you know that half the world lives on less than £5 a day? And a staggering 1.1 billion people live on less than £1 a day. Tragically 3.4 billion people struggle to meet basic needs, like access to adequate water and sanitation, education, and electricity. [2]

These things most of us fail to even consider in our lives. We have warm homes, water in the tap and a fully functioning toilet. Maybe even an en-suite toilet and a third one downstairs? Houses in the UK and USA have an average of two to three toilets. Certainly puts things into perspective, doesn't it?

We seldom take the time to realise just how lucky we are. But please take some time to consider this and then contemplate all the things you should be truly thankful for. I believe this is called the practice of gratitude, of which there is an abundance of reading material to peruse.

We fill our minds with negativity and worries and fail to see all the many (sometimes simple) things we *do* have in our lives: a warm bed, clothes on our backs, loving children, a car, a house, a dog, a friend.

Try to think of everything in your life that you are thankful for, but more importantly, recognise how lucky you are to have those things.

I've always considered myself to be a positive person. Glass half full rather than half empty. And because of this, I've always considered negativity to be well…very negative.

I used to think we must do all we can to wipe out negativity from our lives. We must be positive in all aspects of life and in everything we do. Mustn't we? I have read that by deleting all things negative, and by not having any negative thoughts, then we have indeed managed to find true happiness. I believed that was the only way to be happy: by working on the assassination of all things negative.

It's no wonder that we beat ourselves up with the aim of working towards this impossible state. Because it is *impossible* to murder negativity. Being negative is just as normal as being positive. It's more "normal" because it's a million times easier to be negative than positive.

Once I realised that negativity was just a part of my mind that needed to be managed, I felt like a huge weight had been lifted. Damn those personal development books that make you strive for what is ultimately impossible! Unless you're the Dalai Lama or some super spiritual being on a higher plane (not many of those folks about in Manchester, that's for sure).

An exercise I have done many times with the various teams I have worked with explains this perfectly. It's best to do this on a Monday after a weekend break. Divide the group into pairs, and ask them to sit facing each other.

For the next five minutes, only one person speaks. They are tasked with telling their partner what they did over the weekend. However, they can *only* be positive. They can't use negative language. Just the good stuff, please!

It's fascinating to watch this social experiment unfold. It usually starts well, for about 30 seconds. However, when we say something positive, we usually end with all the things that didn't go well. For example:

> *"Well on Saturday we took the kids to the beach, it was a hot day, and we swam in the sea."* Now, usually what we do then is say what went wrong. *"Billy hurt his foot on a rock, and started screaming, it was totally embarrassing. We then went for lunch and all the places to eat were full, so we ended up just buying a sandwich. I was absolutely starving. The traffic on the way home was awful, took us four hours to do a two-hour journey. I missed my favourite TV programme. Got a migraine so went to bed early."* And so on.

Yes, we can talk and talk endlessly about what went wrong! Now let's try a different outlook on life:

> *"We went for lunch early as Billy cut his foot, but he loved being carried around for the rest of the day. We ended up having a sandwich on the seafront, the view was amazing and the sun was so warm on my back. I felt alive. On the way home we sang songs and played games, it was a pretty long journey, but we had fun. On Sunday I*

> *watched my favourite TV programme on catch up. Had an early night ready for work today. It was a great weekend!"*

When tasked with speaking in only a positive manner, people just can't seem to think about what to say. They want to default to the negative. Try it; it's super hard and takes focused work to not speak in a negative way.

As I became more aware of negative and positive speech, I started to recognise that some people only have negative things to say. On a break at work, colleagues were talking negatively – about their peers, their families, their car, their situation.

Very few times did I hear a 100% positive conversation between two people. Through my new awareness, I started to catch myself being negative and stop. Just stop. Let's just stop being so negative all the time. But my goodness, it became exhausting listening to people with this newfound knowledge.

Another challenge I used when working with people was at the end of the day, I would give them a simple assignment. I asked them to count how many red cars they saw on their way home and coming into work the next morning. That's it. Simple. I always get some very strange looks as people leave the room at the end of their working day. But they usually play along.

The next day I would get everyone together again. "Can anyone tell me how many *blue* cars you saw?"

What? Moans and groans as people reminded me that I asked for red cars. "Yes, I know but how many blue cars did you see?"

The purpose of the exercise is for people to recognise that there were many blue cars, but they were just not looking for them. There could be twice as many blue cars, but you only usually get what you're looking for.

The red cars represent negativity, and the blue cars represent positivity. Our minds have been conditioned over many years to search out the negative. The positive is there, but we don't always see it. Sometimes we just don't see it at all.

I know that many people continue to think I'm crazy after my red car and blue car exercise. However, many people have had a "Eureka!" moment when reflecting on how their minds work. It takes effort to see the many positive things that happen around us. When we have had an extended period of difficult times, we just don't see the positive at all.

But it is still there and always has been. The challenge is reconditioning your mind to recognise it.

I find when things have been very hard for me, the simple task of looking for one positive thing each day refocuses the mind. It can be something as simple as someone letting you go before them in the supermarket queue. Or pulling up to the traffic lights when they turn green. The more you search out the "good stuff," the more "good stuff" you will see.

As a parent, I always encouraged my boys to look to the positive. At dinner each night, I would ask them. "So, what was the best thing about your day?" This simple question every day focuses the mind on the positive. Some days it's hard, and you must dig really deep to find one positive, but this searching process for the positive is a fantastic life skill your children can carry with them through their whole lives. And hopefully, they continue to do this with their children. Certainly beats talking about everything that went wrong today!

So, negativity is not the devil, it's an important part of life. However, it needs to be finely balanced with the positives. You *will* have negative thoughts.

Don't beat yourself up about having them, it's normal. Just balance them out, and if possible, overpower them with the good stuff. Embrace your negativity, but most importantly, *manage* it.

One final note on negativity: If you do the work, you will maybe find people in your life who are negative 80-100% of the time. If you can't help them with this, then maybe limit your time around them.

Find people who help you to feel good and live with a positive mindset. Remember positivity breeds positivity. Negativity also breeds negativity. Wisely choose whom you wish to spend your time with.

Chapter 5
Superhero Single Mums

Yes, I became a single mum when I decided to leave my husband. Yes, it was my choice. And yes, women all over the world become single mums for many varied reasons. The worst of these reasons is the sad loss and death of a parent. Each reason has its challenges; however, putting aside the reasons, a good majority of the issues that single mums face are very similar.

For this book, I will focus on single mums working through divorce. It almost feels like an impossible task to get yourself through the abyss of divorce, but getting yourself and your children through it is a titanic challenge.

Will Mummy and Daddy Get Back Together?

The significant concern I felt with being a single mum in the early days was the tremendous pressure to say and do the right things for my children. But what *is* the right thing to say and do? You must figure that out as you go along, I'm afraid. I have no magic wand for your situation.

Don't doubt that it is natural for your children to desire and crave for you and your ex to get back together, especially in the early stages. There is a period when they try to fix things. In their childlike way, they blissfully console themselves on the idea that one day, you will look them in the eye, smile and tell them, "It's OK, darling, Mummy and Daddy love each other again, and we are all going to live happily ever after."

You need to give them the time and space to handle the reality of their situation. You need to allow them the time to talk and to ask questions – hard questions that you may not be fully prepared to answer (depending on their age). When you can't answer these questions, you must compile a comforting response. Most of all you must give them a place where they feel safe and where circumstances are still as "normal" as they can be.

For about two years, my youngest son would constantly ask if me and Daddy were getting back together. It broke my heart every time. I told him that things were different for us now and that one day I anticipated things would feel better for us all. But I also didn't think we would get back together. That was my truth and I needed him to realise that at some point.

Then one day, out of the blue, he turned to me and said, "Mummy, I think I know why you and Daddy are not together." I gasped, wondering what he was going to say. "Is it because Daddy gets angry?" At that moment, I knew that he'd had a childlike epiphany. He was right, that was one very big reason, along with other reasons I would never share with him. But in that split second, my heart broke because he had seen his dad's angry side. It was that anger I had escaped, but that my son still at times had to endure.

You can work on your own pain, but the torture you feel when your children's hearts are bleeding is like no other suffering. Especially when you feel helpless and powerless. My solution through this was to shower them with my love. So much love that their glass was overflowing with gentle kindness and warm happy thoughts. I put huge effort into them, they became my primary focus; they were, and still are, my everything. And when I was at my lowest point, it was this love for them that saved me from my darkness.

Benefits of Being a Single Mum

Without a doubt, with no significant other in your life, being a single mum has great benefits for you and your children. The most important of these for me was the closeness formed with my children. The limitless time we have enjoyed and endured has made the three of us exceptionally close. I know that I wouldn't have had the connection I have now with both my boys had I not spent many years being a single mum.

We went through the dark days and came out the other side together. We were there to pick each other up when we were down, and to celebrate life achievements when things were going well. We spent hours and hours together, just the three of us, making memories, crying with happiness until our bellies ached and mopping up the tears when needed. Yes, there have been times when I couldn't hold back the tears, when life challenged my very existence. And although I didn't share my deepest fears with them, they saw my struggle and they came to my aid with love and compassion.

Some days when I feel down, I start to think what life would have been like for them if they had grown up in a "normal" and secure married family unit. But in sincerity, I created our own version of a secure family unit. I know they appreciate what I have done for them, and I also know that they won't fully value what I've done until they are way into adulthood, probably when raising their own children. I feel immense satisfaction for what I have achieved, surviving on my own as a single mum through the adversity of divorce.

It's the toughest job for any woman, and of course, I still face new challenges every day. I have had periods with no job, not knowing how I was going to survive putting the boys through school and college. I've not even embarked on the worries that go with getting them through university yet. But I know what I have accomplished to date, and I know that I can manoeuvre whatever challenges I will face in the future.

I haven't purposely *not* been in another significant relationship since my divorce. It's just the way my life has worked out. I've not met anyone special enough to let into my family unit yet. Yes, I want this for my future, as I understand that one day my boys will spread their wings and fly. I aspire to find love, and I do feel that one day this will happen for me.

But know this: *Nothing* can replace the love I have felt from my children, and *nothing* can replace the time we have spent together to build our solid foundation for the future. It was being a single mum that gave me that gift.

My boys have showered me with presents over the years. One year for our holiday, I took the boys to Cape Verde. It was another amazing experience and adventure spent together. On the first evening, we were all exhausted from the journey and trying to acclimatise to the overpowering heat. We had not been there very long, and we went for our first dinner together.

I noticed my eldest acting a bit strange both upon leaving the apartment and as we sat down at the table. The boys then presented me with a box that they had been hiding from me since I packed their bags in England. I opened the box to find a gorgeous silver bangle, it was stunningly beautiful. They said it was a thank you present for taking them on an amazing holiday. They had been planning to give it to me at the end of the holiday, but they couldn't wait a moment longer.

Inscribed on the outer edge of the bangle were the following words: "A mother holds her children's hands for a while, and their hearts forever."

Wow. Just *wow.*

Obviously, it took me a while to dry my tears of utter joy and gratitude for these two bewildered boys sat across me at the table, whom I love abundantly and who loved me unconditionally back.

Below are two of the many poems I have received from them over the years:

My Mum

Have I ever told you just how amazing you are?
And that you're the world's greatest Mum?
Well, you are and these are the reasons why;
Your hugs are the warmest hugs anyone could give.
Your smile brightens the room, making it glisten and glow.
Your laugh fills everyone with complete happiness.
You aren't fazed at the toughest of challenges,
You are Superwoman,
and life wouldn't be the same without you.
You serve food that is fit for an angel,
No wonder they call you a domestic goddess!
Your beautiful eyes shine in the sunlight.
You are my inspiration…and idol…and I love you.
So now you're 21 twice, I just want you to know,
That I don't know how you do it.
But you're a flippin' amazing Mum!

Our Mum

Have you ever met our Mum?
Well, if you have, you'll know that she's

the most amazing person,
With the most amazing heart.
You'll know that she thinks she's the best cook ever,
but in actual fact she's not!
(She's not bad though).
You'll know that she prefers an ice-cold beer to a sophisticated
glass of wine.
You'll know that she has the most warming smile.
You'll know that she's the kindest and
most generous soul in the universe.
You'll know that her favourite place in the whole world is with her
two beautiful cherubs.
You'll know that she hates the Trafford Centre
(with a passion).
You'll know that she hates clothes shopping (I know weird).
You'll know that she doesn't like stress,
but somehow, she can't get rid of it.
You'll know that she always tried her hardest and
strives to be the best she can.
You'll know that she's the person everyone wants and
needs in their life.
You'll know that she's our Mum. That's nice! x

Being Both Mum *and* Dad

Single parenthood is not always a bed of roses. Bringing up kids alone is a massive challenge. My boys fought a lot, and they still do. They argue, they tease, they get each other into trouble, they shout, they scream, they kick, they hit, they drive you to the end of distraction. Yes, that's just part of parenting and life itself. Single mum or not, we all have testing moments of bad behaviour. Did I say moments? I think I meant to say weeks and months…if not years.

When you're doing this by yourself, the trials and tribulations are magnified because you don't have anyone to back you up when times get tough. You don't have anyone to take over when you're at your wit's end. You don't have anyone to comfort you when the kids are literally driving you around the bend. No one to run you a bath and make dinner while the pressure of parenting is taken over by your significant other.

When you're also dealing with the emotions and strain of your divorce, the kids' behaviour is doubly problematic to handle. There are times when your fuse is extremely short and you just don't feel you can take any more.

But you *must* carry on. I've failed in these moments many times – completely lost my temper, got ridiculously annoyed, shouted at the top of my voice and even swore (yes in front of the children – I hear your gasps). But get this: That's normal and we consistently beat ourselves up after these events. Feeling like a failure as a parent, when all we are doing is just endeavouring to do our best to get through the day. *Please,* if you are reading this, give yourself a break in these moments. Remove yourself from the situation if possible, pour a glass of wine (try not to drink the whole bottle), try to relax and go back to your children with a calmer outlook. I know, it's not that simple, is it?

The most significant lesson I learnt through this was that it was OK to apologise. In fact, it's crucial that you learn to apologise – when you are wrong, when you have lost your temper, when you have used "naughty" words. You're teaching your children to apologise too. They learn that you're only human just like them, and it's OK to get mad sometimes. If you're lucky, they learn not to misbehave as much in the future. But they *will* misbehave, and you will continue to get angry. We all have our limits, and families of any kind go through periods of despair due to their children's conduct. Remember, when you're in the midst of divorce, they don't know why they get so angry, just like you don't know why you lose your temper so effortlessly.

Here's the thing about discipline: It incenses me when people say that single mums can't control their children. I have come across this many times. Some people believe that when the man leaves the household, basic rules, discipline and order go out of the window.

"Mums are too soft on their children and they end up being unruly and out of control. They then set about a life of crime and delinquent behaviour terrorising their neighbours late into the night." My blood is boiling!

One night I was having a date at a lovely restaurant, with a guy I had been seeing for only a couple of weeks. I had just started eating my Chinese sweet and sour chicken, when he started spewing his chauvinistic views on how single mums were not able to discipline their children. I was enraged and argued back calmly but with passion for my cause. He continued his onslaught of derogation towards single mums, displaying in full technicolour his bigoted beliefs. So, I did the only thing I could do in that situation. I got up, walked out of the restaurant, and never saw him again. I didn't look back; I was making a statement. However, to this day I wish I could have seen the look on his face. I will buy my own Chinese in future, I thought, and share it with my boys instead.

As single mums, we constantly fight the beliefs of many people in our communities who accept that all single mums are dragging their kids up with no sense of order. I feel that as a single mum, you need to be able to instil more authority, and we usually do. We don't have a "fall-back" partner to help, so we just get on with it. We have more time to devote to talking to our children and showing them the right way to handle life's challenges.

So, the next time you find yourself coming up against these assumptions, I recommend you cut these people out of your life. They bring you nothing, they put you down, they want to keep you down. Surround yourself with people who empower you to be the best YOU and the best parent that you can be. For single mums, the monumental and most significant part of our lives is being a parent, and it is because of this that we make bloody great mums.

Things You Shouldn't Say While Little Ears Are Listening

I touched on this earlier and I feel it's supremely important, so I want to go into more detail on this subject.

It is imperative that you don't talk unfavourably about your children's father.

Especially when there is even a small possibility that they can hear you. I know it's so tempting to have a dig, particularly when you are receiving so much grief from your ex-partner.

But their minds are so fragile and nothing good comes from this. Discuss and vent your thoughts and feelings to close family and friends. It's essential that you have an outlet for this, for your own sanity. But do it away from the kids. And if your friend is at your house and you think the kids are playing nicely; believe me they will be listening to every word you share about your divorce, primarily when you mention their dad.

After you have put them to bed at night, make sure they couldn't possibly hear your telephone conversation where you verbally despise your situation and the hatred you feel for your ex. Yes, I said it. Hatred is what I felt at certain points on my journey. I'm not proud of that now, but it was my reality for a long time.

So, considering that, what do you do when you hear spiteful comments from the mouths of your children that your ex has been saying about you?

You do nothing.

It's a hard lesson and it takes resolve and strength. However, once you discover that you have absolutely no control over what your ex-partner does and says, the easier your journey will be. Likewise, you also can't control what your children hear from your ex's friends and family. But once again you are powerless to control this.

The only thing you can ever have full control over in this life is your own thoughts, feelings, and actions. Being in control of these things is, for most people, extremely difficult. Most of us can only strive to live like this. But even the endeavour to do this is a great step forward.

It's a natural reaction to chastise, and get your revenge: "An eye for an eye, two can play that game." This is especially true when your emotions are running at full speed and overflowing with negativity. Learn to rise above it. It will take a while and sometimes you will fail spectacularly; other times you will succeed and enjoy the benefits of taking the high road.

Take a Break

I did mention that you need to give your children your time. On the flip side of this, you also need to give yourself a break occasionally too.

It's just as important to spend a little time away from your children to recharge, change space, and feel like an adult again. It helps them to become more self-sufficient when you're not around, to trust in other people's safety and care, but most importantly it means they value your time and devotion. Give them the opportunity to miss you a little and to value you more. Quite often we neglect ourselves. As a parent you still need downtime. Even if it's something as small as having a quiet cup of coffee at your favourite coffee shop. Costa Coffee has many times given me a sanctuary to piece my head back together. And they do a fantastic cappuccino!

For separated parents in many cases, this time is given to you in the access arrangements put into place. Once you get over the horrific experience of not having your children around, you can focus on yourself in the times when your children are with your ex. I had this for about one year and was so distraught when they left, that I never got to a place where I had value in this time. Following that year, I had my eldest 24/7, as only my youngest would visit his dad. So, for me, getting time away from being a parent was extremely difficult. My mum didn't live nearby, and babysitters were expensive. Despite restrictions, you need to try to get a little time away where possible. You and your children will benefit greatly from this.

One of the benefits of having my eldest 24/7 was that I understood the value of having 1-to-1 time with each of my children separately. The dynamic changes when it's just you and one of them. They don't have to share you with their siblings, they get all your love and attention.

Doing activities with your children individually has immense benefits, but it's something families rarely do. Having a shared experience or hobby with them separately is fantastic. It's difficult to do, and by default, I had this time with my eldest naturally. It was a little harder to get it with my youngest, but still possible. Make the most of the times when one of your children is at a friend's house, a party, or a sleepover. This is your opportunity to give more of yourself to your other child. It becomes even more difficult the more children you have, but it's certainly something to strive for. Give it a go!

Don't Sweat the Small Stuff

It was a winter's day in early December, and I had arranged to meet up with Carol, my late dad's partner. She had been like a second mum to me, and my boys adored her. Carol and I had been through a lot together, especially through Dad's cancer treatment. We were super close. After he died, we both realised that my dad in his dying days made us both promise to always be there for each other.

We were meeting in the coffee shop of a large bookstore; it was a Sunday afternoon. The boys were being very difficult, as children do, and I was stressed. They wouldn't sit still, and I was exasperated. I was in the early difficult stages of my divorce so I wasn't exactly in a great place, more existing at that time than living, I would say.

Carol looked me in the eye, held my hand and simply said, "Don't sweat the small stuff, Angela." Those words have stayed with me until this very day. She was right. Why was I getting worked up about the boys not sitting still? They were children at the end of the day. It was causing me more stress by how I was reacting to this and many other situations.

"They will be naughty boys at times but try to let the small stuff go and deal with the bigger 'stuff,'" she said. "You will feel much better if you do that, Angela."

She was right. From that day on, I tried not to stress about the small insignificant things that might have previously made my blood boil. I had enough stress in my life dealing with my divorce. They had enough stress in their lives as we navigated our future together as a family of three. Simply said, don't make a big deal out of things that don't really matter!

If You're Happy, Your Kids Will Probably Be Happy

Mmm...that sometimes elusive and hard-to-pinpoint happiness that most people aspire to have.

It's difficult to assess what happiness is. Happiness is so many different things to so many people. To some, it's not going hungry for the day, or it's having a roof over your head or the feeling of being safe. For others, they believe they will only be happy if they win the lottery or have a few thousand pounds in the bank. For others, it's knowing they are loved, appreciated, or content in their lives. Some people never know the feeling of being happy. Happiness is something each person must define for themselves.

One thing I do know is that you need to work on your happiness for your children. How can they be happy if they see you sad every day? This can be the most challenging thing to do, and although I advocate showing your children your true feelings, endless sadness, depression and low moods are a recipe for disaster for your children.

I know it's hard to be happy when your world is consumed with divorce or many other challenging things we face as adults. But you can work on your happiness and you can strive for happiness. Or you can crumble month after month in front of your kids. I know which option I prefer. Remember, they see you unhappy, they feel even more unhappy. They see you trying to see the happiness in difficult situations and you're teaching them to do the same. Now that's a life skill. If you only teach them this in 18 years, then that's really saying something; that's a parenting accomplishment right there.

When you're having your darkest days and are struggling, dig deep and try to transform the moment or day into one of happiness. That's a powerful life skill they will remember and hopefully replicate for their children.

So happy parents = happy children.

Parents who work through the pain towards happiness = children who will also work through the pain towards happiness.

Be in no doubt of the pain your children feel, especially through divorce. Never diminish their pain, just because what you're going through is 100 times worse. When you smile, your children smile. When you laugh, your children laugh. When you relax, your children relax. When you let go, your children let go. When you're sad, *your children are also sad.*

<u>Happy Teenagers</u>

I can't speak of parenting in this book without a few words on teenagers. The teen years are arguably the most challenging time for parents. Most parents will tell you the difficulties of managing teenage hormones and behaviours. That said, teenagers bring a new dimension to parenting never experienced previously. This is where they grow beyond your abilities, at times both in knowledge and especially in stamina. This is the time that you learn many things from them; it's a time when they can walk further than you without needing to rest. They can beat you at any sport and they are able to easily do tasks you struggle with. For example, working your mobile phone or fixing the TV when Netflix won't work!

Teenagers are amazing and beautiful, and seeing them develop and grow into adults is a fantastic privilege. There is a world of opportunities and activities that you are finally able to do together. Holidays can be more adventurous and daring, and enjoying these experiences really can bring you even closer.

And once you've gone through the difficulties of the teenage years (and there will be many of these), you get to witness the fruits of your labour since the day they were born. There is a saying: *Give me a boy until he is seven, and I will show you the man.* As teenagers you start to see their values coming through, and their sense of right and wrong. You get a glimpse of the attributes they will carry forward into adulthood. This, I understand, can either be amazing or super scary, but on the whole, it makes you immensely proud of what you've achieved. The most important achievement in life is holding your children in your hands for a short while and being able to hold them in your heart forever.

My advice when handling the difficult teenage years is that no matter how awful, destructive, and painful it gets, no matter how badly they treat you, they must always be able to know in their hearts that you still love them, and you are there for them. It's so easy to use harmful words in frustration and to feel like a complete and utter failure as a parent. You try to figure out what is wrong with them, where you failed them, and what you can do to help.

You do this by loving them and by supporting them as much as they will allow. You help by sometimes saying nothing. You help by letting them go through this dark period knowing that they *will* come out of the other side. You help by trying not to ask them what is wrong. Because many times they don't even know what is wrong. You help by putting your arms around them when you want to punch them in the face. Yes, I'm sorry to say it can get that frustrating, but know that this is normal, and it will pass. *It will pass.* Your actions here are most important. If you react badly you may cause rifts and trouble that will leak into their early twenties and even beyond.

I also advise that although you may ask for guidance from friends, doctors, and counsellors, only you know what is right for your child. And sometimes you don't. But don't feel pressured into acting in a certain way on the advice of others. I did this at times and it really didn't help. My mum was the best counsel at that time, and many times. She would say, if you don't know what to do, do nothing. Of course, you may need to intervene if you feel they are at risk, you have a responsibility to keep them safe.

But you also need to give them the space and time to figure things out for themselves. Smothering them with too many rules and punishments will only have the opposite effect. It will cause them to fight against you even more. Balance is key.

There is light at the end of the tunnel. Don't beat yourself up, you have done nothing wrong. You still love them, and they still love you. That is all that matters, and love will see them through the dark days.

As a wise, old proverb says, "Just when the caterpillar thought the world was over, it became a butterfly."

Chapter 6
All Things Legal: The Beginning

"You never know how strong you are, until being strong is the only choice you have."
– Unknown

I appreciate that many people manage to navigate the murky water of divorce without the need to set foot in a courtroom, or even a "mediation" session. And for that, I salute you. Obviously, this is the preferred option and I truly believe that you should, at all costs, try to come to an agreement and avoid the trauma that the legal system brings into your life. I say this because I have been to hell and back throughout this process.

However, there are times when this path is sadly unavoidable. When it's impossible to communicate, agreeing on even the simplest of decisions seems hopeless. Had I known at the very beginning that over the next five years I would be in a courtroom a staggering eight times, I certainly wouldn't have believed it. And what I anticipated was going to happen in court was in fact very different and much more frustrating and upsetting than I could have even imagined. Once you go down the legal path, everything becomes excessively serious, formal, confusing, devastating and exhausting. Get the picture?

That said, I would not be where I am today without walking that bumpy road, because in this process you must fight. You fight for your children, for what's right, for your freedom, for your future; and you fight to regain your power as a woman and a mother.

The whole system is completely new to you; it's a learning experience that has many unexpected twists and turns. I started out acutely naïve, as I presume most people do. I believed that if I was doing the "right thing" by my children and I didn't want to be unreasonable, it would be quite easy. I had no absurd requests, I just wanted to agree to our terms for the future. In fact, what I learnt is that "right and wrong" and "truth and honesty" have no place in a courtroom. Not for me anyway. You've heard the phrase "innocent before proven guilty"? Well, in "family" court the opposing side can say anything about you, your character and your motives to make their case stronger and paint you as a bad mother. So, there you are faced with an environment of lies and deceit, a full-on battle that feels like a futile uphill struggle every single day.

Up to this point, I had been at war with only my ex. Now he had an ally to cause me pain, and between them they almost destroyed me. His solicitor was a woman, whom I later found out had no children. She was a formidable force and the only words I can use for her are "an absolute bitch." I admit that she was extremely good at her job and had no scruples in doing everything needed to undermine me, bring me down, and cleverly insinuate that I was the worst mother and human being in the world.

My ex had obviously done a good job feeding her with lies about me and my character. She monopolised on that, and over time she had me pigeonholed into a cruel and selfish woman, who only cared about taking my husband to the cleaners. Over the years I came face to face with her in a battle of words many times. I even have a nickname for her that my friend gave her when she accompanied me to court one time. She was categorically shocked by the way she treated me. We call her "Fish Face"! In some ways, that brought a little lightheartedness to a very dark situation. I would daydream about sending a dead trout in a fancy box to her office when it was all over. I would imagine the look of horror on her face and the stench surrounding her. Clearly, I would never do that, but the thought of it was strangely amusing to me.

Over time I came to hate her with a passion. She filled me with fear and dread, which I surprisingly always managed to contain in her presence. I wasn't going to give her the satisfaction of knowing how much she shook my bones with horror. I remember times when her letters would be waiting for me on the doormat when I got home from work. I would recognise the logo amongst the bills and junk mail. I wish I could have put her letters in the bin with the junk, but this was a time to face all my anxiety and overcome my worst nightmares. My heart would sink every time a letter arrived, as I knew that her words would destroy another small piece of me.

It took four sessions in court to agree on arrangements for the children and our finances. I believed it was all over, but sadly found myself back in court after a one-year break over issues with the children. So, I became quite an expert compared to most people I knew. As you can imagine, the costs involved in this were huge and rocketed out of control. What I am most proud of in the whole process is that I represented myself for six out of the eight sessions. I will explain later why I came to do this. Although it was a lot of pressure, it gave me a *voice*. How could I fight "the bitch" if I was not allowed to speak? It was extremely empowering to be able to speak out when I felt that I had been wronged. And Fish Face hated that.

Let's Start at the Beginning

I needed an attorney. The only involvement I had had with a solicitor was when I was moving to a new house. That was *not* a pleasurable experience: forever chasing the status of the sale while paying fortunes for the privilege. But this time was different, it was about emotions and children, rather than bricks and mortar.

I can't really advise you on how to choose a solicitor, only to say that the two I used were recommended by friends. For the record, just because someone is endorsed, doesn't mean they are suitable for you or your family.

It's important to note here that before any family matter goes to court you need to go through a "mediation" service first. I believe this was put into place to reduce the number of couples who "have to" go to court. It's where you and your ex sit down in a room with a "mediator," and you try to come to agreements. I do believe this works for some couples, however, it was a sheer waste of time for me and only served to delay the process. We had two mediation sessions at an independent solicitor's office, costing £300 per session. In preparation for the first session, we were asked to complete a rather large document which I spent many hours doing, only to find out that my ex had come completely unprepared. That was £300 down the toilet. I hated wasting money like this as I would rather spend my money on my boys. Little did I know at this point that I would spend thousands of pounds on legal matters over the next few years.

In the first mediation session in June of 2012, we spent most of the time arguing about access for the children. Since we had split the previous October, we had not been able to negotiate a rota that satisfied everyone. My eldest son (who was two years old when I met my husband) had grown up knowing him as a father. (His biological father walked out of his life when he was just six years old, and had seen him only randomly before that.) By now he was 11, so to him my ex was the only father figure in his life. But their relationship was strained at times and visitation was difficult for him. He was happy to go but not for long periods. He also didn't want his brother to go alone, so he was very torn in the situation. He wanted to be with me, but he also felt responsible for his brother.

You see I was always the peacemaker in the family, and now when they saw their Dad, I wasn't there. I wasn't there to calm the situation down or to be the voice of reason. I wasn't there to stop the anger from escalating when they misbehaved. That killed me. These details didn't come out until much later when my eldest finally broke. He was so unhappy that he had to stop going. It was difficult because his brother, who was six at the time, couldn't understand why. But my ex was making his life a misery, emotionally blackmailing him to get back at me. My ex knew that hurting him was the best way to cause a great amount of pain for me. And it seemed at that time that anguish was his only goal.

In situations like this, you have to accept that you have absolutely no control over what happens at your ex's house. You have no control over the rules that are set or the boundaries that are put in place (or lack of boundaries for that matter!). That said, if you seriously feel the environment is not positive and is having a severe detrimental effect on your child, you have to act. I know this can be difficult. Seek the advice of your legal representative if you can. Write down your concerns. But try to do this in a balanced way, not a vindictive way. You must stress that your main concern is for the child and their welfare. It doesn't matter if the "other side" can't see your good intentions. What matters is that you *have* good intentions.

I want to note here that sadly, many women especially use their children to hurt men, like making up stories and refusing contact. These vindictive women only make it harder for those of us who act with good intentions. Yes, it's a minefield, and yes this process is tricky and will cause you significant stress. Increase your self-care in this period! But, if you are fighting for your children, you will be astounded where you get the strength from.

As we had very complex child issues and financial affairs to resolve, I needed help. So, I had my first appointment with my new solicitor to start the legal process. I had no idea what to expect. He was a gentleman in his late 50s. I was led to a very formal and stuffy room where he was lodged behind a dark, hefty, and old-fashioned wooden desk. Questions, questions, questions. There were many questions as he tried to decipher what my situation was and what course of action we needed to take. I remember getting very upset, it's painful telling a complete stranger about your breakup when it's all very fresh and raw. It's an open wound, and I used most of my energy in that session either crying or holding back the tears. I remember being emotionally drained at the end of it, but I also felt a sense of relief that I now had someone to fight my corner too. Or so I thought.

This was lesson number one: Be careful who you entrust the outcome of your future with. And be doubly careful when children are involved.

In hindsight, it should have been me who asked most of the questions during that session. I would try to find out what motivates the person who is representing my best interests. How do they feel about divorce and children? What are their personal circumstances? Do they themselves have children or have they been through anything similar? What is their work history? But I didn't do this, I felt totally out of my depth in his office, struggling to speak and even breathe.

In March 2012 I issued a petition for a divorce, and my solicitor made a request for a *Decree Nisi*. A Decree Nisi is a document that confirms that the court doesn't see any reason why you can't divorce. If the judge agrees, the court will send you and your husband a certificate. This will tell you the time and date you'll be granted a Decree Nisi. After the Decree Nisi has been granted, you'll have to wait at least six weeks before you can apply for a *Decree Absolute* to end the marriage. However, legal processes take many months and sometimes years, so it would need to be a simple divorce to come through in six weeks.

In June and July, we went through the mediation process without being able to resolve any of our issues. A petition to court was made to agree on contact arrangements for the children in September. It was now just under one year since the split. This petition was compiled by "the bitch," who said that I had suddenly decided I wanted to spend more time with my children and therefore wanted to reduce her clients' contact. She made this sound like I had not been bothered about contact previously, that I was happy to have regained my "me" time and social life.

The reality was that in the early days, I had struggled with childcare and I had no option but to ask my ex to collect them from school on certain days. When he did this, he refused to give them to me, and he insisted they stay with him for the night. So, in the early days access was evenly split but this had a terrible effect on both boys. It offered no stability, and they were just backwards and forwards all the time. This was my first taste of the bitter medicine Fish Face administered to me on many occasions: twisting the facts to paint me as an evil, selfish mother.

Soon after, my eldest had decided that he could take no more and access for him ceased. This was heart-breaking for him; but because he was in such a bad place, it was a necessary step. His schoolwork had suffered terribly, and he became withdrawn. On days or weekends when he was "visiting his dad," he would try to return home to me on his bike for short periods or spend time at friends' houses to make it more palatable. This all came out in distressing conversations I had with him around that time. The nights were starting to get darker, and I was concerned about him being out in the dark, so I explained that when the evenings were dark, he needed to be inside at my ex's house as it was too dangerous to be riding the streets on his bike. When I had this conversation with him, he broke down in tears. He used his bike to get out and about so that he could spend as little time with my ex as possible. I had to do something but I knew it would be a difficult conversation, so I arranged for a letter to be sent from my solicitor, explaining that my eldest needed some space as he was emotionally in a very bad place.

Surprisingly my ex seemed OK about this, and it was another three years before he had any contact with him again. So, the fight for access became all about my youngest, and about me trying to keep my new family of three as close as possible through the turmoil.

There were copious letters of requests and settlement suggestions between solicitors. These would filter down to myself and my ex, and then we would respond to our respective solicitors, who would write to the opposing solicitor. And the whole absurd cycle would start again.

Each letter was filled with an ever-increasing number of venomous lies and outrageous requests. Agreement seemed hopeless. Common sense and fairness did not prevail. Reading the letters back to write this book, I am still in disbelief at the content. It's still painful and shocking to read.

Family Courts

We finally had our first date in court and it was to try to make access arrangements for my youngest son. My mum came with me for moral support and my solicitor was waiting for me in the lobby. Of course, my ex was there with Fish Face. We were both ushered into separate consulting rooms. What pursued was a comedic backwards and forwards of both solicitors. They would come together to discuss the boy's arrangements. Then my solicitor would return to me with information and suggestions, and the same for my ex. This charade continued for a while when it slowly became very clear that my solicitor didn't understand my situation at all. He certainly didn't grasp the needs of my children or why I had to say no to some of the ridiculous ideas and suggestions that were coming from the other side.

You see, my eldest son didn't want to have *any* access, and my youngest son (who was my ex's biological son) was still happy to go. However, he really missed me and his brother terribly, so going for long periods frequently was causing him a huge amount of distress. I was always happy for access; I had never denied access for my youngest. My boys were really suffering, but nobody was listening to me.

I was trying to make the bitch and a narcissist see sense, while my solicitor didn't even have a basic understanding of the needs of children. With no agreements being made, it was then time to go into the courtroom to face the judge. Each solicitor gave a summary of their client's wishes. I had to sit there in silence and listen to lies – colossal and destructive lies. It was a total shock. How could anyone lie in court? Especially a solicitor? How could she speak about me like that? She doesn't know me. I was helpless to defend myself as I couldn't speak. And to make things worse my solicitor did nothing to defend my honour. He just let it all slip by. I was incensed. How could this happen?

The judge then made a summary and spoke to myself and my ex like we were adolescents, urging us to think of the children and come to some form of reconciliation. Goddamn it, I was there *because of my children*. This was not some idle fight of a woman scorned. This was me fighting for the best outcome for my boys.

The court was adjourned and the saga of "backwards and forwards" between rooms and solicitors ensued again. Each time my solicitor would come back with ridiculous requests. He just didn't get it, he just didn't get me, and he certainly had no understanding of the impact of these requests on my children. My mum couldn't believe the farce of that afternoon. She wasn't allowed in the courtroom, but she observed my idiotic solicitor fumble his way to nothing.

It felt hopeless to be backed into a corner, and I was forced to agree on temporary access arrangements until our next day in court. It was not the outcome I was expecting, my youngest was forced to go to his dad's every other Thursday after school and not return until 5 pm on Sunday.

I remember these times so clearly: On a Wednesday evening he would become irritable and depressed. Not because he didn't not want to see his dad, but because he didn't want to spend the best part of four days not seeing me and his brother. He continued to be passed between me and his dad every few days. It was hard for him when he was leaving me but now, he was leaving me and his best buddy too. It was heartbreaking. It wouldn't take a lot to make it more palatable for him, even beneficial for him, but all my suggestions fell on deaf ears and were immediately refused. The judge set another date to attend court and made recommendations for how we could "agree." Agree! That seemed impossible.

You see, I falsely thought that what happened in court is that each side made their case along with their reasoning, and if you couldn't agree (which, let's face it, is why you're in court), then the court would decide on arrangements, whether that was for finances or children. But no, in my experience, the court is just a very expensive way to facilitate further negotiation. And because it's costing you so much money you are backed into a corner where a decision and extreme compromise must be made. My advice to you in this situation is to try everything you can to negotiate in the mediation stage if possible. This is by far the easiest route. However if you do find yourself in court, have a good long think beforehand about what different options you could suggest on the day that *you* would be comfortable with.

Rank these options in order of your preferences. That way you will be organised to navigate the stress of the day from a considered point of view. Your solicitor (or yourself if you're representing yourself) can then state the number of options you've put forward and that they have all been refused. This will go in your favour. That is far better than trying to negotiate from a view of extreme pressure, in the moment. I guarantee you, your partner will *not* have done this.

We had a new court date set and we could at last go home. I felt extremely frustrated with my solicitor. The bitch had won this fight and she absolutely walked all over him with her harsh bullying tactics. Just before we parted for the day, I asked my solicitor if he had his own children. He only had a stepson, with whom he admitted to having a very difficult relationship.

So, there you have it: the question I should have asked that day in his office that smelt of dusty old law books. He wasn't even a biological father. No wonder he couldn't understand my passion for my children. He also showed more sympathy for my husband's lies rather than believing in me. They shared common ground being troubled stepfathers. Or should I say, having both failed at being stepfathers.

I can't describe how lonely and despondent I felt after that first session in court. I had invested my money and time in a solicitor whom I now realised was unable to help me. What should I do? It was now early December, and our next court date was set for the 13th of February. There was no time to get another solicitor on board and up to speed, and what if it happens again? Who would be able to represent my feelings and my situation with care, conviction and passion? Nobody knew the details of my situation and what had happened on this journey as comprehensively as I did.

The answer was staring me in the face: The best person to represent my children's needs was ME!

I decided to represent myself in court that cold February so that I had a voice, so that I could defend the lies and so that I could speak out when the facts were displayed completely inaccurately by Fish Face.

I fired my solicitor and he sent me a bill for almost £3,000. Yep, that's what it costs to send letters and spend an abysmal day in court. I was so aghast I asked for a full breakdown of the costs. To my amazement, one day in court cost me £1,009 in fees. He charged me £215 in travel expenses, when his office was just 20 miles from the Court Building. My heart sank as I wrote with gritted teeth what was to be the first of countless cheques over the next few years.

I did appoint another solicitor, this time a lady who was again recommended. She had much more sympathy for my cause, and *hallelujah, she understood*. She helped me prepare the various formal documents needed for a session in court. I told her I wanted to represent myself in court and she supported that, being at the end of the phone if needed. Just for the record, when you represent yourself in court you don't have to pay for their exceedingly expensive "time" for the day. That's a saving of hundreds of pounds and even thousands of pounds for a day's work. So, for me it was a no-brainer: I knew my children and I understood what they needed and why; I needed a voice; I needed to defend my honour; and I was saving money too.

On Day 2 in court, my very good friend (the one who masterminded the nickname Fish Face!) came with me for moral support. This was the day that I would confront this woman on my own for the first time. Instead of my solicitor meeting with her and then coming back to me, she had to confront me directly. She had no "middleman" to deal with, she was forced to come straight to the horse's mouth with her ridiculousness. I was ready, my children were at stake and I was *strong*.

I pulled on some inner strength I had lurking deep inside and I faced her with my conviction and my passion. I wouldn't let her walk all over me. I had the knowledge to contradict the lies she had been told and she hated me for being able to do this. I knew I was getting under her skin. She thought I would be a walkover, but I was like Goliath that day.

We then went into the court to face the judge. I was armed with pen and paper to make notes of her lies so that I could defend myself when it was my turn to speak. I stood up and confidently made my case. I exposed her lies and put the record straight and it felt wonderful. I could have been 10-foot-tall that day. You see when you represent yourself, you don't know what is acceptable in court or the formalities, which means you can get away with going off protocol. I could say things that a solicitor would never have said and that they wouldn't have known because this was my life, and I was living it.

The rest of the afternoon was spent negotiating the terms of the final Court Order for access for the boys. It was a painful and laborious task, but I stood my ground and eventually, we came to an agreement. Of course, I had to make compromises, but in the main, I was happy that I had a good result for the boys. Fish Face was seething, we were there until the very last minute of the day. It was a small win for Ang Allan-Burns and her boys. Yes, the justice system stinks, what happens in family court and what the solicitors can say and do is disgusting, but I had fought and won. For today at least.

When I arrived home in the early evening, I felt empowered. I learnt that I have a steel-like grit inside me, one I would need to call on many times in the future. Knowing it was there gave me a new sense of belief. I've got this, I thought. I didn't, of course, but feeling like I was superwoman for the day was amazing. That evening I seem to recall drinking a lot of wine in celebration of my victory.

Money and the Courts

Now that we had a court order (or as I call it a "very expensive piece of paper") that sets out when each parent had access to my youngest, we could move onto the financial side of things. The two issues are, rightly so, kept very separate in court proceedings. So, I was sent a letter with a court date for the "First Directions Appointment." Unfortunately, due to my ex being on holiday, the court had to reschedule, so it was further delayed for four months, just under two years after the initial split and the fourth anniversary of my father's passing. It was also the day before I was to move out of the family home due to its sale a few months previously.

During this time, it was necessary for the family home to be put up for sale. The house was sold in two days, which flung me into an infinite panic to find a rented property and to clear the house ready for a move. Moving to a new house with two small children, while representing yourself in court, holding down a full-time job, and managing being a new single mum…yep. That's tough.

The move date was set for the day after court! We had already waited a further four months for this date. To delay again would have been crazy. I went to court and the very next day, we moved to a new house. Funny how life's big events all come crashing down on you at the same time. Dealing with divorce, moving to a new house and bereavement at the same time. What a nightmare. I was surrounded by boxes and legal paperwork. No wonder I drank a lot.

With a little bit of knowledge now under my belt, I knew this session was to review the case, try to negotiate and then adjourn until all parties have had time to prepare further documentation set out by the judge.

So, despite the house move, I decided once again not to take my solicitor when it was just a formality, and nothing would be decided on the day. My solicitor helped me again with the paperwork, of which there was a mountain of it. I remember many nights sat on the floor in my living room after the boys were in bed, with paperwork scattered around me in an organised mess. Pen in one hand, a glass of wine in the other.

When dealing with finances we had to complete a full "financial disclosure." This is where you complete the largest document you've ever seen with all your financial information alongside copies of bank statements, pensions, etc. It's a huge undertaking putting this together and it leaves you feeling somewhat violated. Every purchase you have made is shown in black and white for everyone to see. From how much I spend on my weekly shopping to where I buy my knickers. Your whole life is in that document. You get a copy of the same that your ex and his solicitor have prepared too. Unfortunately for us, there was so much time between the first and second court date that we had to reproduce the document a second time, so I can honestly say it was a document that I could happily have set fire to on more than one occasion.

This was now my third session in court, and my second representing myself. This time, however, with my friends at work and my mum looking after the boys, I was going it alone. It's a strange feeling, going to court alone: You feel a little exposed not having anyone to comfort you when things get heated. I had to be strong *again*.

However, I felt a new confidence after the last time. The people who work in the courts had all been extremely understanding. Due to the lack of legal aid now in the UK, more and more people are finding that they have no option but to represent themselves. For me, I knew I could hold my own. If I could contain myself from getting upset, I would be fine. Even later down the line when I had some harrowing experiences, I always managed to be strong and hold it together. I also found that in the main, the judges were kind and considerate (except one. More on that later). The judges would explain what was needed in simple terms and provide direction in a kind and considerate manner.

This third time in court was, as I had thought, a formality. The usual discrediting of my character and finances ensued, and once again I had a voice that I used eloquently in the courtroom. We had very different viewpoints about what *was* and what *was not* part of the financial package to be split. My ex had a very large pension and I had a sum of inheritance money from my father's passing the previous year. I had suspicions about other financial shares and trusts that I believed had been syphoned away; unfortunately, I could never prove the existence of these. My boys also had inheritance money that my father wanted them to have. My enormous mistake was that this money had not been put into trust. It was and always had been kept in an account in my name. The judge had read the pre-prepared documents that my solicitor had helped me to compile then she listened to each side of the argument. We were then asked to go away and compile further evidence for another court hearing that was set in three months' time.

The period between the third and fourth court days was significantly burdensome for me. There was fierce fighting and accusations, ridiculous requests for a final settlement that catapulted me into a meltdown of fear for the outcome and for our future. I had two boys to raise and financially I had no clue about how I could do this, considering what was being demanded by the bitch!

Fish Face prepared lists of suitable houses in her attempt to prove how little money I needed to survive and provide a home for the boys – properties that I wouldn't let even my dog live in. It's all so very cruel and hurtful. How could he want me and the children to suffer like this? I knew he loathed me and wanted me to have as little as possible, but why couldn't he see that doing this to me impacted the boys too? Legal costs were spiralling out of control and my solicitor was not hopeful that we would be able to get what we thought was fair in the fourth court session.

In pure desperation, I obtained a second opinion from yet another solicitor. She was a top divorce lawyer in Manchester, so I thought, maybe she could help me. It cost me £252 (that I couldn't afford) for an hour of her time. We sat in her swanky office and I told her the complete story. She gave me hope that I, in fact, should be entitled to a pension-sharing agreement, and that, as I had thought was fair, this should be part of the financial settlement. However, she made it clear that I didn't have the funds to pay her huge fees and recommended I remain with my current solicitor. You see my case was not valuable enough for her to help me.

I recall sitting on the tram on the way home. It was a sunny summer day. I had my head resting on the window, looking out across the skyline of Manchester. I was broken. I had no more fight in me. I was not crying, as there was no "cry" left in me…just hollow despair. To add to my problems at this time, I had also found out that my job was seriously under threat. My company had announced over 1,000 job losses. How would I cope if I lost my job now? I didn't know how much more I could take. But the express train of divorce kept on gaining speed. With the end of my journey not yet in sight, I cried myself to sleep most nights.

It was a few more weeks until the fourth court hearing. My solicitor said we would try to conclude things in this session if possible, and urged me not to go alone. I didn't have the legal knowledge to fight Fish Face this time. It was different when the subject was my children, but this was about the intricacies of the law.

For the first time going to court, I was a broken woman. I just needed this to be over. I had very little energy, my mind was an abyss of despair. I was in a supremely bad place.

Fish Face never ceased to amaze me. However, this time she sank to a new low. She argued that because the boys' inheritance money was in fact in my banking account, it should be added to the total financial pot. The judge didn't bat an eyelid. I had to be silent, but I was seething inside. How could they do this to my boys? How could he want a share in my boy's inheritance? It was hopeless, despite me having a copy of my late father's will; it was viewed as family money to be shared in the divorce. Remarkably, because my father had died while we were married, my inheritance had to be shared. But for reasons that still escape me now, my ex's significant pension could remain his in total. This seemingly was because he had been building this fund since before we were married. My argument was that my father's inheritance had been building since the day I was born. It just all felt so wrong, so unfair, so bitter, so brutal, so callous and cold-blooded.

We adjourned and I sat in the consultation room with my solicitor in disbelief. I hopelessly questioned her as she admitted it was fundamentally wrong. She explained that the only way I could fight this was to take it to the next stage and go back to court maybe once, maybe twice, maybe more times. This would involve me having to be questioned in the witness box by Fish Face.

At that moment, I knew I was done. I could not do this again. I had nothing more to give and nothing more to fight with. For the sake of my survival and mental state and because I had to go on living to be there for my boys, I decided it was over. You see this period became so challenging for me, that on several occasions I decided I couldn't continue with life. I wanted to end it all. It seemed the only way to stop the constant pain of this nightmare. My only way out. I was saved only by the love of my boys, they were and always had been my "why." I couldn't leave them. They saved my life.

All that was left to do was to decide the percentage split of money. This was to be done in the weeks after this session, so

I could at last go home. I have no recollection of the journey; I just remember my mum putting her arms around me and sobbing into her shoulder. I was relieved that it was all over (or so I thought at the time); however, this relief was overwhelmed by an emptiness. It took a few days for it to sink in that I didn't need to read or prepare any further legal documentation. I didn't need to think about it every single moment of the day, and slowly, step by step I wasn't consumed by it.

Divorce Absolute: **A Scrappy Piece of Paper**

We had dealt with all the issues around the children and our finances. I had moved to a new house while in the depths of a legal battle, and going to hell and back. Now, all that remained was to wait for the official divorce papers to land on my doorstep.

For weeks, months, and now years, I had imagined the day when I would finally have the piece of paper that confirmed I was divorced from the man who had caused me so much agony. I had imagined the pure joy, excitement, relief and celebration that this would bring. For what seemed like an eternity, I had waited patiently for it to arrive. I had heard stories about people having divorce parties, a celebration with close girlfriends who had shared the journey, popping champagne to their new-found freedom.

I waited for the letter to appear and the anticipation faded. Then, one day when I came home from work, totally oblivious to the momentous occasion before me, I saw it.

THE letter.

The very thick envelope with a huge document nesting inside. I opened it in my kitchen. This was it, that hollow feeling returned as I read my solicitor's full summary of the events of the last few months. Thereafter her final invoice, and my heart sank. This was the final miserable payment to her, money I could have spent travelling the world with my boys, wasted topping up her probably over-inflated bank account. I felt sick.

Then there it was, my *Decree Absolute*. What I had fought so valiantly for. I expected a certificate of some kind, but it was only recognisable by those two depressing words on the bottom right-hand corner in tiny print.

It was not a celebration for me. It was like a death, the final scattering of the ashes of a time I was trying to forget ever existed, and that I thought I would never recover from. I did pop a bottle that night, not to rejoice, but to mourn. I drank until the hollowness drifted away, then went to bed, alone.

It had taken two long years and five months to get to this point. Month after month of tears, disbelief, anger, despair, devastation, headaches, sleepless nights, dark cloudy days and wine-infused evenings. I'd lost my home, some friends, some family, and thousands of pounds.

However, I had my dignity, the love of my children and a heart that felt happier with every new day. I believed it to be over.

But it wasn't.

The Recovery

Despite having to endure another house move, a few months of calm followed. By now, I was having regular counselling sessions that had started sometime between court visits number 3 and 4. I was over the worst of my dark night and I was slowly building myself up again. It was tough because I didn't know who I was. My life had been devoured by this one thing.

I forgot who Angela was. I didn't know how to be her. I suppose what I did to get through was to try to be the best mother I could be. But I had neglected myself. I knew I had to "find" myself again and become the woman I was previously. The person I was before I met my husband. But that was 10 and a half years ago now, she was a distant faded memory. How do you do that? They say that time is a great healer, and I suppose I hoped that in time I would be OK. I had to believe that.

As I struggled through, we continued with life getting through the days, me trying to mask the fact that inside I still wasn't over this damn thing. I did everything to forget the fact that I was still deeply affected inside. That year my boys and I did many fun things together. I had always made sure that we were busy having adventures, but now we could enjoy activities together in the sunlight instead of under a muggy black cloud. The dark cloud that had followed me everywhere. It was a time just to enjoy each other and be happy. We had two trips away, one to Southport and the other to Anglesey. These were the first trips where we all totally relaxed. They were amazing, fun-filled days out in the fresh air. We went go-karting together and tried horse-riding for the first (and last) time. We rode our bikes, and had barbecues on the beach.

My eldest turned thirteen and my youngest turned nine. The boys had brilliant birthdays and life was starting to get better with each new dawn. My youngest would see his dad every other weekend and then either one or two days during the week. We stuck to the court order and it worked. He missed us, but I had fought for him to return at 3pm on a Sunday so he knew he could still enjoy time with me and his brother before school on Monday. This worked. It was worth the arguments with Fish Face!

Obviously, my eldest and I had a lot of time together, as he had not seen my ex for about one and a half years. It still upset me that my ex didn't seem to care about him. He had been his son for nine years, knowing him as his dad. But he relinquished the relationship so easily, without even a fight. I knew this saddened him but there was absolutely nothing I could do to take this pain away from him.

He would say to me, "I don't have much luck with dads, do I, Mum?" He'd had two so-called "dads" turn their backs on him. It was heartbreaking. So, my answer to this problem was the same: to adorn him with as much love, affection, kindness and stability as I could. We came to cherish our time, we would go ice skating on a Saturday together or to the movies, or just cuddle up on the sofa, eating sweeties and watching his favourite films. He had me, and I hoped I was enough. It was still painful for him, but I washed some of this away with love. One day I know he will make an amazing father, because he has seen the worst of dads, and he would never inflict the same pain on his own child.

After the *Decree Absolute*, we had six months building ourselves back up again – me trying to discover myself and failing. But there was a reason for this that I couldn't have known at the time. I now know why it wasn't over for me, why I couldn't move on. The universe couldn't let me get over this yet.

Because it wasn't over. In fact, it all started again…but this time it was even more heart-rendering than it had ever been.

Chapter 7
All Things Legal: Final Stages of Court

In September – now three years since the split – everything changed.

There are many parts of this story that I can't speak of in a book and are too personal to me, my boys, and my ex. I will do my best to give you an overall impression of the following 15 months.

That's 450 days of pure anguish, devastation, despair and disbelief. The strain and mental torture throughout this time was more than the three of us had ever endured in the past. Looking back at that time, it was extremely painful for all of us; every moment of the day was laden with hardship and constant challenges. It would see me go back to court four more times. Yet again, I had to pull on a strength buried inside to get through it. I'm reminded again of the saying, "You never know how strong you are until being strong is the only choice you have."

This period was all about my youngest. He had become very distant and distressed. His behaviour was deteriorating, something wasn't right. In September, he told me that he didn't ever want to see his dad again. He had just returned from a week with his dad, and it had been littered with anguish and arguments. As I have explained before, my ex was very strict, and my son had just decided that enough was enough. I suppose when he was with his dad, the environment was very different to when he was with me and his brother. I went to see my ex to find out what was going on, trying to be calm and understanding.

He admitted to hitting our son on the odd occasion. I said that it was never acceptable to hit a child. My son's story was quite different. He told me that he was dragged upstairs, locked in his bedroom and hit on more than a few occasions.

Over the next four weeks, I tried to work hard with both my son and his dad to help resolve the problems. Through talking and building bridges, he eventually decided to give his dad another chance. I knew that a complete breakdown of their relationship would be destructive for them both long-term. We had a meeting at my house and sat around the kitchen table. My ex was very apologetic and promised not to hit him again. Eventually, I arranged for them both to meet up in McDonald's and I waited outside in the car so that my son felt comfortable. All was good, he was happy and having spent a few weeks with no contact, I believed that things would be calm again.

A few weeks later, when he was once again with his dad, I started to get messages from him via his iPad. He wanted me to collect him, he pleaded for me to get him "out." Many things happened that night, and eventually, my only option was to call the police, as my ex refused to speak to me and let him come home. I was going out of my mind, but at 1am, the most wonderful and understanding police officer brought him home. The three of us were deeply upset and unsettled. Over the next few days, it became apparent that my son's mental state was in a bad place. An incident occurred that led me to speak to the school and to get social services involved. I took my son to the doctor and they did a referral to Children and Adolescent Mental Health Services (CAMHS).

He became a different child. He was angry most of the time and had many severe outbursts. He would throw things and hit me and his brother repeatedly. He would shout and scream, which would turn into uncontrollable crying. He was violent and out of control, and I struggled to deal with him. It was a strenuous time for all of us. My eldest – bless him – tried to help me manage his brother's behaviour, but I didn't know where to turn.

In the moments when he was not having an outburst, we talked. I tried to piece together his feelings and to help him manage his turmoil inside. He told me that he was frightened that I was going to persuade him to see his dad again, as I had done previously. I was devastated. I made a promise to him that I would *never* force him to do anything he didn't want to do. If he didn't want to see his dad, then that is what I would fight for, for him.

My ex didn't understand the mental state that he was experiencing. He thought that I was encouraging him not to see him. He refused to believe that this was coming from our son. I told my ex that it was going to take time. He needed help, he needed counselling and at some point, I hoped we would get through this. I asked him to be patient, but I guess it was difficult for him, as access had now obviously completely stopped.

I was in breach of the court order. So, his answer was to get "the bitch" back and into our lives. He applied to the court for the enforcement of a Child Arrangements Order. By this time, my son was receiving counselling, but his mental state had not improved. He was still extremely concerned that he would be forced to go back. I had no option but to do the right thing by my child. His needs were the only thing that mattered, and I had to fight for him.

Following that incident in November, every day was a new challenge. Living became all about my youngest and trying to manage his behaviour. I was at my wit's end. My referral for him from the doctor didn't come through until May, so I had no professional help until then. The CAMHS people were helpful and recommended a fantastic book that you read with your child to help them manage their anger outbursts. They suggested that I contact Relate, a provider of relationship support in England, and ask for a qualified child counsellor who could help him with the issues he faced with the separation. These sessions were extremely helpful. He was too afraid to go into the sessions alone, so I went with him and sat quietly in the corner. It took a while for him to open up, and when he did it was heartbreaking. Slowly we managed to work through it together and the outbursts became less frequent. At last, we were making progress. Many months went by, and my youngest insisted that he still wanted no contact at all with his dad.

Then I was served papers to attend court in September.

Here we go again. I had hoped that my time in court was over. I couldn't avoid it, however, unless I was willing to force my son to have contact. I had made a promise many months before that I would never do this. I had no option but to face Fish Face again. It was the last thing I wanted to do, but I did this for my boy.

Throughout that year in conversations with my youngest, my intention was always to get him to a place where hopefully, negotiations could take place and some form of contact resumed – perhaps where I or someone else was present initially. I knew that for a nine-year-old never to have contact again or through his childhood would not be a great outcome. I wanted to get to a place where his dad would be different. I had hoped that this period without contact would be a massive wakeup call to him, and that he too might get some help in dealing with his anger. I wanted my son to understand that the rest of his life was a long time and that maybe one day he would be able to see his dad, but in different circumstances where he felt safe.

We didn't go to court until the following September. It was now four years since we had split up – four long years and I was here again. Still doing this shit. I knew that I was the *only* person who could convey in court what my boy needed and what he had been through. I knew every sordid detail. I had lived this trouble and strife for the past year, so this time I didn't even involve my solicitor. This meant I would have to compile all the legal documentation for myself. Google is an amazing friend when faced with this. You can search for samples of documents that you can copy and download. Many late nights of research ensued, along with conversations with charities that provide legal help via the telephone.

I was ready; deep breaths, Ang. Being ready for court, or as ready as you can ever feel, gives you some confidence for the day. I know it's scary, and if you didn't feel a little apprehensive then that would be very odd. But know that you've done all you can and that you will have the strength to face the day with power. Because the power will come to you. You will dig deep in these moments and rise when needed. You may break afterwards, but at the moment you will be OK. I would recommend you devise some Words of Power or affirmation for these days in court. Keep saying these words to yourself over and over again. This will help to calm the nerves and feed your subconscious mind, "You've got this."

I didn't know about this when I was in court, but I use Words of Power now in my everyday life. I say something like, "I am powerful and I am strong." "Today I am a formidable force." "I am calm and I am here for the good of my children." You don't have to believe these words, but say them to yourself repeatedly. It's probably more powerful if you can come up with your own version. What do you *need* to say to yourself in these moments to give you strength and power?

During my research, I realised that it was indeed possible for a friend to accompany me inside the courtroom. I had read many papers and stories about representing yourself in court by now and stumbled across something called a "McKenzie Friend." This is where you can request another person to assist you in court, not as a lawyer but as a friend. Of course, there was a huge document to complete that needed to be handed into the court when you arrived. Another good friend of mine came to support me and was my McKenzie friend for the day. It was amazing and comforting to have her next to me in the courtroom. She took notes for me so that I could concentrate on what I needed to say.

Fish Face was furious that I did this. She wanted me to be alone in yet another attempt to break me down in court. She had failed to do this in the past, and I do think now that this had become quite personal for her. She hated the fact that I had stood up to her; I don't think many people in her life had ever done this. Even my first solicitor crumbled in her presence.

As with all first-hearing disputes, this session was a formality. The judge listened to both sides of the argument and as the case was acutely complex, she set out what documentation was needed for a future court date.

I was asking the court for a Non-Contact Order. I explained that I hoped, at some point, my son would be able to see his dad in time and with ongoing counselling. But I wanted this decision to be his. I didn't want him to be fixed to a contact order, so I was asking for the old order to be abolished. I thought that with the evidence from the reports that we needed to gather from the counsellors and the police, this was not an unreasonable request. However, I knew that this was categorically not what my ex wanted. I really don't believe it was truly about access, although I do think my ex wanted to see his son. But more than anything, he needed to win.

Court Date Number 6! Wow

It was my belief that at the next session, the old court order would be dissolved. This made me very fearful. Yes, it was what I needed to do for my boy, but I became increasingly unnerved by what my ex's response would be towards me if that happened. Police involvement had been an occasional necessity since the very beginning of this journey, and I was fearful for my safety. This fear can cause you to spiral out of control if I'm honest. I know I did for a time. I would suggest taking some advice from a Domestic Abuse Charity.

You will find these in all areas so there should be one not too far from you. A quick Google search should bring up a few options. Speak to them about your fears and they should provide clear simple advice. You need to take steps to do everything you can to feel as safe as possible. You still may not feel 100% safe, but by doing this you are highlighting officially the situation you are facing.

After endless nights and yet more research, I decided to apply for a Non-Molestation Order. I wanted to get this in place so that after whatever happened in court, I knew I would be safe. In my home. I wanted him not to be able to come to the house and bang on my windows in anger, upsetting me and the boys. I thought that if he knew he couldn't go near me, I would feel safe. Looking back now it seems unbelievable that things got to that point, but that fear was very real to me.

So, I completed all the paperwork myself, compiled my evidence and went to court *again*.

This was court date number 6.

This time, due to work commitments of my friends, I went alone. There were no discussions before the session, we were ushered straight into court. The judge was an older man in his early 60s. He was very stern and sombre. I thought that by this time nothing could surprise me in a courtroom, but I was severely wrong. Despite my evidence of incidents in the past, and because my ex had not actually caused me any bodily harm, it was not possible for him to grant my wish. I was incensed. I argued my position and my fear considering our looming court date. But the judge dismissed me. He ordered me to be quiet, however I continued. "So you're saying you're not going to help me? That I have to wait until he actually hurts me before you can help me?" "That's sickening." "Thank you for nothing."

I sat down defeated and I just wanted to leave as soon as possible. He granted me an option to adjourn with "liberty to restore to await further developments." Well, thank you very much. I will give you a ring from bloody hospital, shall I? I didn't say that for fear of getting into trouble. A courtroom is like the worst headmaster's office you can imagine. I didn't look at him, I just walked out in disgust.

Our seventh court date was looming, and I hoped it would be the last. A few days before I received in the post a copy of my ex's statement to court. This had also been sent to the court ready for the hearing date. I recall sitting on my bed, reading it with tears in my eyes. It was good, it was very good; but it was lies, downright lies. The bitch had outdone herself this time. It was so believable. I was the woman scorned from a bitter divorce who had already turned my eldest against her client, and now in my bitter revenge, I sort to turn my youngest against his dad too. She insinuated that I was using him as a cruel pawn in my twisted existence and final game to cause severe pain to her client by ceasing all contact with his children.

It discredited my character and my ability as a mother. Everything that had happened in the past was turned against me, even the police incident the previous November was cleverly explained away as actually being my fault. It was unbelievable, it even contradicted what was in the police report. But it didn't matter, the truth didn't matter. All that mattered to them was their story to win the case. To get what they wanted, not to do what was best for my boy. Why couldn't we work together to get him to a good place in his good time? Why did they have to force all this nastiness?

I was not a bitter, twisted divorced woman using the boys as a weapon against her husband. I was a struggling single mum, trying her best to protect her children. I needed this to be over and to focus on giving my boys the childhood they deserve, not a childhood scarred by years of difficulties with their father and court battles.

Over the next day, I sat down and wrote another statement to the court that I intended to take with me on the day. There was no time to post this now. I fiercely defended myself against the lies and deceit. I said that their statement was far removed from the truth. I needed the court to know that I only act in the best interests of my son, and I have made endless efforts for the relationship between him and my ex to not break down. After about five pages, I ended the statement by saying that at some point in the future, I hope that it would be possible for contact to be reinstated. But this will need to be in my son's own time, and his decision. I said that I have discussed with my son many times that "if and when" he wants to do this, I will fully support him. Whether it's in two or six months, two years or even when he's older. It's only right that he knows this, and I hope that one day when he is more emotionally equipped to deal with it, this will happen.

Armed with my defence statement, I walked into court on my own, to fight for my boy. When you arrive in court, you sign in with the court official. It was just after the lunch period and the waiting area was very quiet, and I waited patiently behind a man who had a few questions. My ex walked in, I noticed him and felt sick. He walked up behind me to wait in line.

In what seems now like slow motion, I turned my head and looked straight into his eyes. In a calm, soft voice, I said, "How can you tell so many lies? It's just all lies." He looked at me and just shrugged his shoulders and smirked. I could feel my blood boil, I wanted to leap towards him and rip his eyes out. Of course, I didn't. I remained calm and looked at him like he was the lowest form of human being on this earth. I gave my name to the court official and handed him my statement to give to the judge, and a copy to give to Fish Face when she arrived.

I took a seat and tried to breathe to calm my nerves. Fish Face arrived shortly afterwards, and she was handed my document by the court official. She disappeared with my ex into a consultation room. She was annoyed. Incensed. She then came over to me and said that I can't do this, I can't bring a court document with me. All documentation has to be submitted to all parties before the hearing. I shrugged my shoulders, hoping she would feel some of the anger I had felt just minutes before, when I was on the receiving end of a shrug.

When we went into court, she spoke to the judge firmly requesting that my counter-statement not be used. The judge, however, knowing that I was not fully versed in court protocol, dismissed her request. She did however give me a good telling off and told me never to do that again, that all documentation must be disclosed prior to the hearing date. I was OK with that. Fish Face wasn't.

All I can say now is that the next 45 minutes were the very worst I had ever experienced in a courtroom. And as you know, I have had a lot of experience. Fish Face continued her onslaught of discrediting my character alongside copious lies. My side of the story was quite different; however, a lot of my content could not be supported by concrete evidence. When I spoke about my son and his mental state over the past year, it was just my words.

Unfortunately, the counsellor would not issue a letter to the court due to the confidential nature of my son's counselling sessions. She would only do this if the court summoned her to do so. Fish Face had found out that I was in the room when he had his counselling sessions, so she insinuated that he was following my wishes and using words that I had fed him. The judge was incensed that I would be in the room. I tried to explain that my son was too scared to do this alone and I was there for moral support. I certainly didn't put words in his mouth. The judge said that he would not be able to speak his truth with me present and that it was ridiculous. She was so awful to me, talked to me like I was some slut of a single mother, scorned and revengeful. I was astounded that she, a woman and maybe a mother, couldn't understand my child.

Fish Face had brought my eldest into the proceedings, telling the judge that I had set him against his dad, and that my poor ex had not seen him for two years. I argued that he had not once wanted to see him, but again I only had my truth and my words. I suggested to the judge that the Children and Family Court Advisory and Support Service, or CAFCASS, speak to him and not just take my word for it. She looked at me and said, "Well if we do that, you must not prep him, you must not tell him what to say."

What?! Did she really think I would do that? She was basically saying that there might be some truth in Fish Face's lies.

I started to feel myself breaking down, and I called on all my reserves to make it to the end of the session. The judge ruled that the case was so complex, and the two sides were so far removed from each other, that she thought neither side could see what was in my son's best interests. She ruled that my youngest should be given his own solicitor to represent his best interests in the next court session. He would also be given his own CAFCASS officer who would work with him to establish his needs and the way forward.

I had to sit there and listen to this woman, who thought and acted like she was God, say to me that I didn't have my son's best interests at heart.

OMG OMG OMG. No words can explain how I felt at that moment. Sitting there alone next to Fish Face and my ex and the judge from hell. Before she ended the session, she gave me that piercing look again and said once more, do not speak to your son, do not tell him what to say, do you hear me? The court was adjourned, and a date was set to return at the end of the year.

I was the first to walk out of the courtroom, continued to walk and walk and I didn't look back. I walked as fast as I could, down the lift and out of the building into the fresh air. I felt faint and dizzy, my head was a scrambled mess. I was shaking from head to foot. I knew I just needed to get home. But my car was parked a long way from the court, as I had been at work that morning. With my head bowed low to disguise my face, I started to walk in the direction of my car.

The Manchester streets were busy with shoppers and businessmen. The cascades of tears were now in full flow. You know the feeling when you're crying, but you have to keep it inside, your shoulders start to shake and you blubber, restricting the noise that's trying to escape. I considered stopping somewhere to gather myself again, but I knew if I stopped, my cries would break out. That journey home is as clear to me now as it was on that day. I had a small tissue in my coat pocket, but within a few minutes, it was drenched.

My nose was running, and I was trying to wipe my eyes with bare cold hands.

Eventually, I reached my car, it was parked in a multi storey car park. I sat in the driver's seat, and for the first time, with no one around, I could let some of my cry out. I didn't stop crying. All the way home whilst driving, I was crying. I was just trying to get to my home where I was safe, and no one could hurt me. Where people loved me. It was the longest journey home, an eternity. By this time, I couldn't keep anything in, balling at the traffic lights. It must have been quite a sight, as I am sure other drivers must have noticed. I had promised my mum that I would call her as soon as it was over. But I couldn't make a call. She was waiting for me at home.

Still dizzy and still crying, I arrived home and got out of my car. My mum was waiting by the window, she must have known. I hazily walked to the door and she opened it and looked at the state I was in. I fell to my knees. I was safe, I could let it all out now, and boy did I. Luckily my youngest was on his iPad in his room with headphones on. But my eldest who was well aware of what was happening came to comfort me. They both cradled me, while I cried and cried until there was not a drop of water left in my body.

Eighth and Last Time

I was left shell-shocked and dismayed. This soon turned to anger. Anger not against Fish Face, but against the judge. She obviously had her prejudices and preconceived ideas about me, as a person and a mother. How could she get away with doing this? But in that courtroom, you can't fight a judge. Who do you complain to? And if I did complain, surely that would not be good for my case. It would make me look like a woman who wasn't happy with the court process, a difficult woman who would fight against anything. That would play straight into Fish Face's hands. She already had me down as an unstable, revengeful woman. I was between a rock and a hard place.

All the while my conversations with my youngest son remained supportive, and I never once spoke negatively about his dad. I continued asking him how he felt about seeing his dad in a safe environment. I did this because that was the right thing to do for my child. I was being accused of cruelly setting him against his dad, but all I ever did was to try to support a resolution. I'm not taking the moral high ground here; I'm just trying to point out how unfair it can be. Through this awful backlash against you, it's imperative that you don't lose focus on what you're trying to achieve for your children. Of course, deep down I wanted him to know what I was suffering on his behalf, the abuse I had to suffer in court, and that it was all his dad's fault. But that's not what responsible parents do.

When I considered the impact of him having his own solicitor, I was actually happy about it. I needed help to fight Fish Face, and if his solicitor talked to both my boys the truth would come out. I also couldn't reason with the bitch or my ex, and now the judge was clearly against me!

My son had an appointment to see a lovely lady called Valerie, who worked for CAFCAS. I'd had a few conversations with her, but she wanted to speak to him, on his own. She came to the house where he felt safe, and she had a clever way of putting him at ease. I urged him just to tell her how he felt and to be honest. I told him that everything would be OK and that this was just a part of the process.

I did not prep him! However, I confess I did listen behind the door. The session went well, and it was such a relief that he found the strength to tell her what had happened and how his dad made him feel. He spoke about his dad losing his temper and hitting him on his "bare bum." He said that he didn't want to see his dad because he was frightened he would hit him. Valerie asked him what would need to happen for him to give him another chance, and he said he would have to "not get angry anymore." She said that she was going to speak to his dad about this. There were lots of other things that were discussed that day, and I can't describe how vindicated I felt that he was able to speak his truth to someone whose opinion would be listened to in the courtroom. She made a report to his solicitor and that made me feel a little better about my next visit to court.

Over the next few weeks, my youngest started to improve. His anger was under control and both me and his counsellor were happy with the progress. One day while snuggling and chilling out on the sofa, he struck up a conversation about his dad. He said, "Mummy, I've decided to give my dad a 'third' chance." He had already given him a second chance. It was now just over a year since he had seen him, and enough time and healing had passed. I was happy about this and had always said I would support him with this decision; however, I was a little concerned about his safety.

My Final Day in Court

I spoke to Valerie to give her the news. As we were in the middle of a bitter court battle, now everything had changed. We made a plan that he felt comfortable with, starting with small sessions, and building from there. I was cautious, but I did feel that my ex would be on his best behaviour. Let's hope that continues.

There was still the matter of court to take care of, so yet again in December we went to what seemed like a second home now to finalise the arrangements. I was very clear that despite contact now being resumed, I still wanted him to be the one who had control over when he went and for how long. I didn't want him (or me) to have to go through this again if it all went wrong. Before we went into the courtroom, me, Valerie and my son's solicitor agreed that this would be the best way forward. Having read the CAFCAS report, I think that Fish Face felt it was impossible to disagree. This is what I had been fighting for: control for my son. And I was very happy with this arrangement.

When it was time to go into the courtroom, I was somewhat nervous, knowing the monster of a judge and remembering how she made me feel in the previous session. This time it was super quick. The judge was only concerned with the fact that the problems had been resolved and contact had been resumed. She didn't go into any further detail.

What I *did* want from this session that didn't happen was for the judge to say that I was right. That it wasn't lies. That I was the person who had been instrumental in working closely with my son and his counsellors to get him to this point. It was because of *me* that we were in this good place, because I *am* a bloody good mother. But I heard no words of this kind, I heard no apology. Nobody even spoke of his discussion with Valerie that vindicated my case. I had won, I was happy about the outcome for him, but it didn't feel like a win. It never does. There are no winners when you take matters to a courtroom.

Very slowly over the coming days and weeks, he rebuilt his confidence with his dad. I was super nervous when he eventually returned to full-day visits and even overnight sleepovers. I think that because there was no court order, my ex knew that if he went back to his old ways, he could wave goodbye to any future contact. So, it worked. I don't know this for sure, though I do believe that my ex might have had some counselling. He became very different and much more understanding. He had endured just over 12 months of no contact with his son and despite the lies betrayed in court, he knew deep down inside that this was his fault. When he closed his eyes at night and was alone with his thoughts, he knew.

We even managed to get our relationship to a good point where we could discuss the boys without difficulty. It was an amazing transformation from where we had been. More importantly and significantly, after three and a half years, he wanted to try to rebuild some form of a relationship with my eldest. I was astounded. I knew this would be a challenge for him, but I also knew that it would be good for him to get to a good place and finally put all the pain of the past to bed.

In the years that followed, my relationship with my ex was always strained and difficult. He would take any opportunity to hurt me or make life difficult. I just learnt to manage it more effectively over time. And I do believe that this will always be the case. There are many challenges and frustrations that will probably continue to the day he dies…or the day I die. While that makes me very sad, my boys have come to understand this too and have accepted it. I have no power to change this man, I only have the power to fight for my children.

My legal battles went on for years and were the most challenging part of my life to date. Would I do it all again to get the same result? Absolutely. Would I get more help and support emotionally? Absolutely. You have to keep going, but ignoring the signs that your physical and mental health are both being affected can be extremely dangerous. I urge you to seek support through the legal days of your divorce – even if you think you don't need it.

I didn't seek professional help until after I reached my lowest point. In hindsight, I *needed* help way before I crashed to my depths. The toll this period had on me was devastating and took me many years to recover from. Don't do what I did; self-care is the most important part of getting to the other side of the Big D word.

If you're constantly feeling anxious, depressed, out of control, or uneasy even, please get help. Talking through what you're going through really does help. A professional with experience in these situations can give you strategies for self-care, mental strength and stability. And let's not forget the toll this takes on your children. We can be so immersed in our own desperation we fail to see the effect it's having on them. Yes, we try to mask it, but they can see it. They can see the strain on your face, the tone of your voice, and how you lose your temper quickly and easily. There are some amazing child counsellors out there who can help. In the UK, Relate has excellent child and family counsellors. If you don't go down this route ensure you give your children the space and safety to be open about their feelings. Encourage them to talk to you.

CTFO – Chill the Fuck Out!

I do hope you take my advice about self-care. We all know as parents there are always going to be times when your kids drive you to distraction, whether you're going through a divorce or are happily married. So how can you deal with these inevitable times which are a completely normal part of parenting?

I do love a good acronym. I came across this a few years ago and now it sort of stuck with me. I seldom say it out loud, but I use it often when speaking internally to myself. CTFO, Ang. CTFO, ANG!

I will admit to being a bit of a stress ball at times. Maybe some would say highly strung, excitable, nervous, sensitive or dare I say it, occasionally unstable. Stress comes in many forms and what I have realised over the years is that stress begins with the very small things quite often. These small things build up and you can easily hold onto them instead of letting them go. Then your stress levels grow and intensify. And that can go on for many years. If you then experience something comfortably recognised as stressful, like moving to a new house, divorce or constantly squabbling children, it all piles on to manifest one big stress bomb. These days, I work hard to try not to stress about the smaller, more insignificant stresses of life. But like many things already discussed, it takes constant work to keep that bomb from growing to nuclear capacity.

There are many ways you can CTFO. Firstly, you must recognise you need to CTFO! How you speak to yourself, and what you say to yourself in these moments are a huge factor in how you deal with stress. That's why CTFO has helped me to remember to stop, breathe, rationalise, and relax. Breathing has been instrumental for me in difficult moments. Deep breaths in and deep breaths out. It's only breathing but it really works to calm the mind and body. Meditation and mindfulness are also practices I have dabbled in. You need to find what works for *you*. When I feel like everything is getting on top of me, I like to go for a drive, pick up a drive-through coffee and just be. Be still. Be calm. Just be.

When I have more time, I go for a long walk, and if I really need to CTFO, I drive to the sea. Watching the sea on a quiet piece of coastline whether the sun is beaming, or the waves are crashing gives me a new sense of purpose. It calms my soul. Find your calm. Find your stillness. Rest your mind in whatever way works for you…and CTFO!

Listen and Be Guided

One day a man was drowning in the water. A boat came by and the captain said, "Do you need help?" And the man said, "No thank you, God will save me." Then another boat came by, and once again the captain said, "Do you need any help?" And the man said "No thank you, God will save me. Then the man drowned and went to the gates of heaven, and he said to God, "Why didn't you save me?" And God said, "I sent you two big boats, you dummy."

I absolutely love this tale. It sums up perfectly the need to listen to both the little voices inside of you but also the big screaming sounds of the universe. Depending on your religious beliefs you may refer to this as God or God like. Or maybe you believe in a guiding force or destiny. You may not have any beliefs of such things and I certainly don't profess to know exactly what they are, but rest assured, they are there if you listen.

We've all felt times when we are immensely compelled to do something. Well, that is it. You must follow these urges and grasp the helping hand that is being offered to you. Most of the time our minds are so busy with life that we find it hard to hear these impulses. Or we quickly dismiss them and get on with our daily lives. I've had these impulses come to me repeatedly and kept pushing them away, because I am too busy, too tired or too involved with the course of action I've set for myself. When the universe is shouting at me to change direction, I've not listened and spent many years ignoring guidance from above.

However, eventually the God force I think becomes exasperated with your dismissive behaviour and makes life so terrible that you have no option but to listen. Big change usually comes after a period of big pain or devastation. We've given up and don't know which way to turn. Then we are ready to listen. And we do because we feel we've exhausted every other avenue.

Having been through this cycle many times, I now realise it's just easier to keep an ear on the voices inside. To quiet the mind to ensure that you're open to new ideas and changes in direction. To learn not to dismiss ideas and thoughts immediately. I find it helpful to ponder on these for a few days. Sometimes they develop into actions or further considerations, and if you're lucky, that develops into a whole new plan. All you must do is listen and trust that you are being guided by whatever force you choose to believe in.

When you have no idea what to do, do nothing. Just be still. Try to quiet your mind and listen. The worst thing you can do is to busy yourself with desperate action. Do nothing and keep doing nothing. Until something comes to you and you find your way. Don't live in chaos. When you feel like the road you're on will swallow you whole, stand still. When you're struggling to feel anything at all, just hold on. It will come. Just focus on you, on getting through the day. Be patient.

Destiny is a wonderful concept and one that I absolutely believe in. Our paths are marked, and we are absolutely where we are meant to be at any given time. That's not helpful when you're not in a good place. But following periods of obscurity comes clarity. A new way forward. There are two important days in our lives: the day we were born and the day we understand why. We spend years sometimes searching for our why. In these moments of listening and waiting for our destiny to reveal itself, we can find it.

Don't be afraid to start over. It's a chance to build something better this time. And never apologise for leaving a situation to make yourself happier. We don't find our strength and grace because everything worked out. We find it because shit went wrong, and we handled it. Hour after hour, day after day we worked through it and manifested a better life for ourselves. So be strong when you are weak. Be brave when you are scared. And if all you can do is to quiet your mind, do nothing and listen. Then that's a step forward, don't underestimate its power, let it happen. Trust in its magic.

Chapter 8
Surviving Access

Just about every separated parent has heard, or will hear the words, "I hate you," or "I want to live with Dad (or Mum)." If you've not heard them yet then brace yourself: They're coming.

This is normal, especially when, as a good parent, you discipline your child in the right way. Often, they will resist discipline, and this is also normal. You and your little ones will soon realise that these words are usually said in anger – anger towards you for putting your foot down. These words are rarely what the child truly wants to happen. Call it an idle threat against you, like putting them on the naughty step when they refuse to comply and run around the house like a crazy chimp.

It's also normal for children to resist going to see the other parent at times. This can be for many reasons – maybe they feel unwell, or they're just comfortable and can't muster the strength to swap houses.

Maybe they're having so much fun playing with their toys or their friends, that going to Dad's isn't the most attractive activity at that time. Although difficult, you must do the right thing and direct your children to get up and go. Sometimes being quite "matter of fact" about the situation helps. It's not up for discussion and it's just what they must do.

There are however times when you need to sit up and listen to your little ones when the situation becomes more serious. If a child becomes overly sad and distant when it's "hand over time," then something more significant is likely to be going on in their unworldly head. It's extremely upsetting watching a child go to a parent against their will.

Situations of crying, screaming and angry outbursts are all too common and severely difficult to deal with for both parents. If God is on your side, you will have a partner who understands these difficulties and can talk to you and your child about what's going on. In my opinion, these situations can only be dealt with effectively when there is good communication between each parent, and between both parents and child.

When communication is fractured and there is a lack of understanding, these situations can become about, "It's my time, they have to come with me." They can quickly escalate into a presumption that you are revelling in your child not wanting to see the other parent. But the truth is, it's heartbreaking to watch a child suffer this turmoil. I have spoken to many friends about this and watching your distressed child leave you with tears in their eyes is *not* what any good parent wants to see.

There are so many emotions running high at these times, that it's practically impossible to decipher what's going on. But if these instances are a recurring theme, then drastic action may need to be taken. Having had both of my children refuse to have contact at different times, each for valid reasons, I had no option but to defend and support my children. Their emotional well-being is far more important than any court order.

Yes, it's very messy and you will be branded as an evil mother using her children as a weapon and refusing them access. They will get sympathy from friends and colleagues, "Poor me, she won't let me see my children," but that is irrelevant to you. You just focus on the needs of your child.

It is sickening that some mothers *do* refuse contact for no good reason. Or their reason is to cause pain and abandonment to the other parent. That is just cruel and, in my view, psychopathic. It doesn't help those of us who refuse contact with only the best intentions at heart for our offspring. Unfortunately, you will be branded with the worst of womankind. In my experience, most mothers want good and happy contact. They want their children to have solid meaningful relationships with their dads.

Even when our situation was at its worst, I knew that the way forward was to work at resolving the issues, and for the "no contact" to be short-term. A few months, maybe a year or two, whatever time is needed for faith to be restored.

I appreciate patience is required in this very delicate situation. It is only communication that heals the understanding of this. When the understanding goes out of the window, the situation can become desperate.

My son worried that his dad would approach him on the street or go to the school to collect him. He was so scared that I arranged with the school for him to leave via a different exit, where I would wait to meet him.

It sounds ridiculous now that they have a positive relationship; however, that is the place we were in. So instead of my son riding his bike to school and back again, I now had to take him to school and be there to pick him up before the school bell went. To do this, I had to take a job on reduced hours as it was no longer possible to protect my son and work full time. This was what was needed, and this is what I had to do to ease some of the fear. I had no family help, no family who lived nearby and could take some of the burden. By doing this my son started over time to feel safer. It is in this safety that he became more relaxed, and with talking and his counselling sessions, over time he started to think more positively. His anger became easier for him to control.

These changes don't happen overnight, but you just need to keep your head down, be as supportive and loving as possible, and know that you will come out of the other side.

For me, there was no understanding of this process from my ex, which is why we ended up swimming in the murky waters of the legal system again.

When children are extremely distressed, I don't believe they should be forced to do anything against their wishes. That terrible night in November, I remember saying to my ex, "Just let him come home for tonight, and we can sort it out tomorrow." He was distinctly distressed. When he refused, I remember very clearly saying to him, "If you don't let him come home tonight, he might not want to go back to you." He hadn't seen his son for over a year; however, he caused that situation, it was his doing. Yes, he blamed me; however, it was I who resolved the situation in the end. *He* caused it that night, with his behaviour and stubbornness.

Access for stepchildren is a whole different matter indeed. My first son was just two years old when I met and married my husband. My eldest couldn't remember a time when he wasn't there or a time when he wasn't just his dad. He was more of a dad than his biological father, who seldom saw him and walked out of his life when he was just six years old.

To me, my children were both my ex's children. We had even arranged for my eldest to change his name, so we all had the same family name. So how come the word "biological" becomes so important when parents separate? I don't know the answer to that. I just know it does. I remember in the early days when Fish Face suggested that I pay my ex for the times my eldest visited his house. It was an idle threat, but it was still a low blow. From that moment, I knew that my eldest was viewed quite differently in this whole affair. As he was a non-biological son, there was no child maintenance payment for him. And I wouldn't have expected that. But to charge me for seeing his son of nine years? Unbelievable.

The only good that came out of him being a stepson is that when visitation became very difficult for him and he desperately wanted and needed to stop going, I had all the rights. My ex had no right to demand anything, which made life easier for me. However, what is more upsetting is that my ex didn't want to make any effort to see him. He didn't want to resolve the problems of why he felt so unhappy when he was with him. He was quite happy to let him go and to focus on his "biological" son. This made me angry; how could he do that to a child? To my child!

In the end, it wasn't about my son, it was about hurting me. It was about using my child as a weapon of destruction. And that weapon was very effective. In fact, it was the nuclear bomb that caused me the most misery and pain.

Stand Up and Fight, for You and Your Children

When you're in the middle of a legal battle, which goes on for months and years, your children go on this journey too. You obviously need to try to keep as much detail from them as possible, they should never become embroiled in the details. However, you must realise that they live with you and they see things. They see the strain on your face. The desperation. The sadness. The fear. Yes, you try to hide this from them, but even the youngest of children feel your emotions and pain at times.

I remember when my first son was just a baby and he had just started walking. I was going through another difficult time in my life. The relationship with his dad had broken down; he drank a lot and became impossible to live with. I was faced with a situation where I had to ask him to leave, especially as I had a baby in the house now. (That's another book that I will maybe write one day.)

At that time, I was made redundant from my job and I also had a cancer scare to deal with. One day, when it all got too much for me, I remember crying on my bedroom floor from pure exhaustion and desperation. My baby boy was in his nappy playing with his toys on the other side of the room. The most amazing thing happened. He went over to a tissue box by the side of my bed, pulled out a tissue and walked across the room, handing it to me with a knowing look of compassion. He was only a few months old. I didn't even realise he had noticed me crying. He was just a baby, but he felt my pain. So, the human spirit and empathy are alive and kicking in even the youngest of our children.

Guilty Mother Syndrome

As you're fighting for your children and yourself, it's your children who give you the strength to carry on. Without them, I'm not sure it's possible to endure what you must go through.

Children have an amazing insight. They seem to know when you need a hug. They have a way of being able to make you smile and even laugh when peace and contentment seem far away. I found that spending quality time with your children helped me through. Putting all my efforts into fun activities helped to bond us together, and to forget about the daily struggle. This gives you the impetus to continue. Despite all the difficulties, you have these amazing little people who can make you feel better, to relax.

As a mother, we feel guilty about many aspects of divorce and what our children must endure. For me, it was my decision to leave that haunted me. I made this happen by speaking out about not being happy. I did this to them. Maybe I should have just been happy with "my lot"? Had I known how difficult it was going to be, would I have done it?

Absolutely.

You see many times I had decided to try to be content with my unhappiness. I didn't want my children to suffer the devastation of a broken relationship. But in the end, I didn't do it just for me, I did it for them too. And as a result, we are all the better for it. Despite the dark years.

That is why guilt should have no place in your heart. You do what you need to do, and as long as you're not being completely selfish and you're doing this for the right reasons, you should *not* feel guilty.

It is because of guilt that we tend to overcompensate. If you're trying to make things easier by showering them with presents at Christmas or birthdays, that's fine. Do what you need to do, just make sure you provide the correct type of discipline along the way.

In our case, my kids and I would delight in doing things that were not possible previously. We would have big messy pillow fights. We'd stay up late sometimes on a school night, enjoying long walks together and buying things that cost over £50!

One New Year's Eve we had a party, just the three of us in the house. We had party food and loud music. The boys and I would jump and bounce from chair to sofa, laughing and giggling. It was such fun and something that would never have happened before. In fact, previously on New Year's Eve, the boys would have to be in bed for their normal bedtime. My ex and I would share one (yes, one) bottle of wine, and probably go to bed before midnight. I remember the year before the split, lying in bed at midnight, my ex asleep beside me. I was listening to the fireworks and the raised voices of intoxicated people outside, singing and wishing each other a Happy New Year. I was far from happy laid there in bed. I was miserable and depressed. I was dead inside. My then-husband had been oblivious to this.

The joy now of being able to do what I wanted for me and my children without feeling guilty, is spectacular. It's empowering to be free when you have been controlled. To live in the moment, without having to comply with someone else's restrictions. I know people who fear this, fear being the decision maker. But independence has many rewards. If you can be financially independent and make your own decisions, you can truly be the person you are deep inside. A good relationship is a partnership, it's give and take. But when you feel restricted, confined, put down, imprisoned…then it's time to make a change.

"If you don't like where you are, move. You are not a tree."
– Jim Rohn

Counselling and Stress

As you navigate the shark-infested waters of divorce, my advice to you is to do as much self-care as is humanly possible. I didn't devote anything to this, especially in the early days. You go into "survival" mode and robotically look after your children as a number one, and then all the many aspects of managing your divorce. Taking time out for yourself, even just to check if you are OK is rarely a focus.

If you're lucky, you will have friends who check in on you, and family members who ask frequently, "How are you?" or

"Are you OK?" And you will say, "Yes, I'm fine." Or you will tell them you're just getting on with it all. Or you will also say, "Yes, I'm good. It's hard but I'm managing."

These are naturally the things we can say to our loved ones, when really, our insides are shattered. You need to honestly have these conversations with yourself. You can't lie to yourself. Ask yourself, "How am I? Am I managing?" Reflect and answer honestly. If you can feel yourself struggling, even a little, this is the time to reach out. Don't wait until you hit rock bottom.

Talking to friends and family members can be fantastic therapy. However, as the months and years increase, you feel less able to continue spreading your misery. And people sometimes become exasperated with your lack of ability to talk about anything other than your struggles. But for you, it's real every single day. No wonder you don't have the time to focus on other things. That is why I would recommend that *everyone* going through divorce seek out the guidance of a trained counsellor. Even if it is a relatively easy divorce, your whole life is transitioning, and finding help with that can have a massively positive effect.

I waited until I hit rock bottom before I acknowledged that I needed help from someone who was trained in these things. If you can find a counsellor who specialises in divorce, then great. However, this isn't necessary. Having someone who isn't invested in you in any way or involved in your life just to help you open up and figure things out is the best form of self-care I can recommend.

It has to be someone who can guide you through, whom you don't feel guilty talking to negatively. Someone to get your thinking on the right track. Someone to ensure you stay on course and don't self-destruct. Someone to help you rationalise and deal with the fear. Having that someone is essential to your recovery.

My counsellor made sense of all my negative thoughts and helped me come up with solutions. This enabled me to make some of the negativity go away.

I remember in one session I was really upset about the financial implications of the divorce. What she uncovered is that the root of this was knowing that I could no longer afford to take my children on a fantastic holiday abroad that year. I felt as though I was letting them down and was a complete failure. My costs were spiralling out of control. Through discussion, we identified that there was little I could do about my spiralling divorce costs that I wasn't already doing. However, she helped me to come up with a holiday adventure for my boys that was truly amazing. It was in this session that I decided to buy a tent with the little money I had and to give my boys a camping experience. This was something we had always wanted to do but never got around to. The following weekend we bought our first tent and what followed was many years of awesome camping experiences.

You see, sometimes it's the simple things that we beat ourselves up about, that we can, with help, find solutions to. These solutions give us the space and strength to carry on. Our camping adventures were times when we could all be free. Especially me. Free from my constant thoughts of doom about my divorce and situation. I also felt so empowered as a woman to do this with them. Alone, with no man to help. I did it. I was super-mum on these trips.

The counselling sessions I've had have helped me to deal with many aspects of my life, including my very difficult relationship with my sister. For over 10 years I had experienced great sadness about our relationship…or the lack of it. I had tried so many ways to have a good, loving relationship with her, and every time I tried and failed, I went through the same set of emotions: failure, pain, hurt and disappointment.

My counsellor helped me to see the whole situation through different eyes, and from that one session, I felt different and no longer experienced the pain that I had inflicted on myself for years. It was like lifting a huge weight off my back. It had nothing to do with my divorce, but it was a great help having one less thing to beat myself up about.

I know that some people are reluctant to talk to a stranger. But you need to try it at least once. Unfortunately, not all counsellors are good, just like in many other professions. And just because someone has been recommended doesn't mean you will have the same experience. So, if you find someone whom you just don't seem to click with, who can't give you a lightbulb moment in your first session, find someone else. You really should in that first session have a feeling that this person understands you and can help you. Pick up the phone today. It is money very well spent. Or get in touch with your doctor or workplace, as they may be able to provide this free of charge.

> *"I stress about stress before there's even stress to stress about. Then I stress about stressing over stress that doesn't need to be stressed about. It's stressful."*

Stress is a state of mental or emotional strain or tension resulting from adverse or demanding situations. The signs of emotional stress are anxiety, depression, irritability, memory and concentration problems, and mood swings. I would say I experienced all those symptoms for 90% of the five years it took for my divorce to be over.

The causes of stress include being under lots of pressure. Facing big changes? Check! Worrying about the future? Check! Not being able to control the outcome of something? Check! Having overwhelming responsibilities? Check! Uncertain times? Check!

We experience all those things to sometimes unacceptable levels when going through a divorce. It's no wonder we are stressed. Accepting stress in your life and recognising it's a normal part of the process is the first good step. However, how do we stop stressing when we have so much stress to deal with? Simply saying I'm not going to get stressed provides little help, though this is a good decision.

There are some things that *can* help: Exercise, reducing caffeine intake, journaling, spending time with family and friends, laughing. Supplements can also help, and I'm also a big advocate of medication if this is recommended by your doctor.

There is a real stigma about taking medication. But if it will help in the short term to deal with huge amounts of stress, then I say go for it. I don't know how I would have coped without my "happy" pills. Not that they made me feel happy, but I did notice a big change when taking them. However you decide to deal with stress is your choice, and you will find many different recommendations on the internet. Most importantly know that you need to manage this increase of stress in your life and the techniques you use will help you throughout life. Because it's not only divorce that's stressful. Moving home, the loss of a loved one, when work goes bad, changing jobs, etc. Life throws many different challenges and how we deal with this stress will have a direct link to your recovery from divorce.

I urge you to pause reading here for a short while. I'd like you to get your journal or some paper. Write down everything in your life that is currently causing you stress. Big or small. Then take a look at your list. Is this stress valid? Is it relevant? Is it time-specific? Is it stress that needs immediate attention?

Does this stress relate to something in the future that might not happen at all?

I'd like you to then rank these stresses in your life – from the worst or highest stress to the lowest. Study your list carefully. Cross out any stressors in your life that you should simply remove from your thoughts. What are you stressing about that is unreasonable and that you can cross out immediately? Decide to remove these from your life, as focusing on these does not serve any purpose for you.

Now, with what you have left, take each stress in isolation. Consider for each one what you can do to reduce this stress in your life. Just one action that you can do in the next 48 hours that will help to reduce this stress. Even if it's just a small reduction. If it's easier, start with the ones at the bottom of the list that cause you the least amount of unease.

What this exercise does is help you realise that some stressors in life are totally unproductive and unwarranted. The things that do cause you the most stress can be reduced with a few simple actions. Don't just think about this, do the work, write the list and take time to discover your actions. It's only by doing the work that you will make significant positive steps towards a less stressful life. Of course, you can't make them all magically go away. You can get your stress list in order and work to improve.

Once you've done this, write another list of all the activities, people, and daily or weekly rituals that you do that help you to feel calmer. Do more of these! Make time in your schedule to ensure you bring quiet and stillness to your mind.

Here's one to try. It sounds mad, but weirdly, works:

Shaking!

When you experience a stress response, your body prepares for action (fight or flight) by tensing up. Shaking allows this built-up tension to be released, helping the muscles to relax. Shaking can help to metabolise and discharge stress hormones, like adrenaline and cortisol, that are released during a triggering event. Your body doesn't speak verbal language, that's why you can't just tell yourself to calm down or chill out in the moment. In fact when people say this to you we quite often get more stressed. So shake it out to destress!

It's so easy to go through life without self-evaluating how you can do things better. We tend to be on the treadmill of life and rarely get off to refocus attention. Try a quick Google of stress relieving techniques. There are many to be found, you just have to find the right one for yourself, your body and your mind.

Meditative Walking

There are many ways to find peace or to quiet your mind to enable guidance. You need to find something that works for you. That could be several different things, like going to the gym or driving your car. I have developed over the years a combination that I find very effective, for me at least.

The mental and physical benefits of walking are well documented. Getting out into nature, and feeling the wind on your face and the fresh air in your lungs are uplifting and inspiring. I love to walk with my two boys, especially in places where there are as few people as possible. Getting out into Mother Nature taking in awe-inspiring views, mountains, hills, lakes, waterfalls…it's just amazing. It encourages us to talk about things we wouldn't normally talk about day to day.

It provided space to explore and be adventurous. My love of walking has developed over a long period of time. If you do this frequently you find that in periods where you don't get out, you feel sluggish and an immense need to soak up all the healing benefits the living world provides.

Walking alone, however, takes me to an altogether different place. It's a gift I give to myself when I need to be at peace and to find my calm. Just the physical aspect of putting one foot in front of another and moving in a repetitive manner is illuminating. This time is 100% for you. No distractions – just you, your body and your mind in total harmony.

I find that it's a great time to think, especially if I have a decision to make. It's a great time to ponder options, but more importantly, it's a fantastic time to quiet your mind and see what pops up for you.

Try it. I've been amazed by the ideas that have sprung into my mind, ideas that wouldn't have come to me at home. Especially if you have a busy home and working life. At home, there is always something to attend to. Out in nature, while walking, you can easily check your phone, but do keep it away in your pocket. Put it on silent so you are not disturbed. This time can be the most valuable gift you can give yourself. Something about nature creates clarity for many situations. And if you find yourself focusing on things you would rather not, then just push those thoughts away. Try to think of absolutely nothing at all. This nothingness is the state where you're open to direction. Don't misjudge this as dead time. If nothing comes, that's OK, you still get the benefits of relaxation and a calm mind.

Have you ever tried to do nothing and to think of nothing for more than 30 seconds? It's practically impossible. But if you can achieve this, you will experience its benefits. One way I do this, especially when I am very stressed or worried about certain things, is to meditate while walking.

I've never been able to fully get into meditation as a daily practice. I seem to manage it for a few days, then slip back into the old habit of not creating the time in my day to do it. I first learnt the practice of meditation very early in life. I was around the age of nine or 10 years old.

My mother had become involved with a Transcendental Mediations group. She meditated daily for around 20 minutes and I remember observing the peace it gave her. The group also did meditation for children, which I became involved with.

For children the "way" that you meditate is different. Children very rarely sit still, so instead of sitting down in a quiet room, I learnt to meditate while doing activities. They suggested walking as good, but it could be anything. Playing or drawing, etc. I was given a mantra to repeat in my head over and over again and did this for about 20 minutes.

I did this every day as a child for a long time and remember clearly how happy and peaceful I would feel afterwards. When I was about 12, I was given a new "adult" mantra and learnt the "sit-down" meditation that is widely practised around the world.

I didn't continue with this daily practice into my teenage years, but throughout my life, I have drawn on this learning and used my "adult" mantra in times of difficulty. It was my way to connect to a higher force when I was desperate or under great fear, stress, or pressure. It calms me; I don't know how, but it does.

One day while out walking alone, my mind was all over the place. Constant worries and frantic thoughts consumed me. So, I just started using my mantra while walking. It took me back to the days when I was a child, walking or playing while quietly saying my mantra over and over in my head. It was amazing. I started to calm down and just focused on breathing, my mantra and my walking.

Nobody knows what you're doing, you just look like you're taking a walk. But it becomes a more focused and peaceful walk.

If you don't have a mantra to use, just say a few words like "All is well" or "Life is good." If a few words are too much, then use a word that you want to feel more of, like "calm," "peace," or "love." It really does work. People who say you only live once are wrong. You only die once, but you live every day. And if doing these crazy little things helps you to live a little better then why not try it? You have nothing to lose.

How Often Do You Worry About Things?

The English dictionary's definition of "worry" is to think about problems or unpleasant things that might happen in a way that makes you feel unhappy or frightened. The word that stands out for me here is "might."

Yes, we worry hundreds of times a week, or even in a single day about things that might never happen. It really is a waste of time and mental energy. It depletes you and is very unpleasant. Worrying is like walking around with an umbrella waiting for it to rain. How ridiculous is that? But we do and will continue to worry.

I suggest you spend some time "consciously worrying." This is where you become aware of what your brain is doing and the mental conversations you have with yourself. This will help you identify just how many times you *do* partake in this nonsense. When a "worry" pops into your head, blow it away and replace it with something good. Think about something or someone who makes you happy and distract your brain for a while. If you practise doing this, you will find that you naturally worry less. Give it a go.

Sometimes however these worries turn into something much more harmful: *fear*.

Fear is a "worry" on steroids. This is when you are frightened about dangerous, painful, or bad things that might be happening or might happen in the future. Fear is crippling. It uncovers feelings of dread, terror, alarm, fright and panic.

People can also experience symptoms of being overwhelmed, upset, feeling out of control and even feeling a sense of death. You can also experience physical symptoms, such as a racing heart, sweating, nausea or dizziness and a suffocating feeling.

Fear has two meanings: "Forget everything and run," or "Face everything and rise." The choice is yours. It's imperative that when you experience fear, especially self-inflicted fear arising from your own thoughts, you learn how to deal with this. Take some time out; it's impossible to think clearly when you're experiencing feelings of fear. Breathe.

The only way to deal with fear is to face them and put them into perspective. What's the worst thing that could happen?

Look at the evidence, what are the chances of the thing you fear happening? Life is about 5% what happens to us and 95% how we respond to what happens to us. Every single event in life that happens is an opportunity to choose love over fear.

Decide to choose love. Yes, sometimes it's that simple. It's a simple choice you make inside your head. Everything you've ever wanted is on the other side of fear. And yes, this sometimes means living at the end of your comfort zone, where life begins, and fear diminishes. Remember that sometimes what you're most afraid of doing is the very thing that will set you free.

It's worth investing some time in this. Make a list of all the things you worry about. Then make a list of all the things you're afraid of. Take a few days to complete your list so that you have everything in front of you on one single piece of paper. Now, put a line through all the things on your list that you are unnecessarily doing. What worries or fears are irrational? Which ones are not likely to happen to you in the next six months? You should have knocked quite a few from your list, as many of these worries and fears *never* happen.

Now, look again at your list. Identify three or four from either list that you feel are holding you back. What can you do about these fears? If you had an endless amount of time, what could you do? If you had an endless amount of money, what could you do? Who can help you tackle these? What actions can you take to ensure these worries and fears go away?

Just the process of working through this exercise helps you clearly see, rationalise and identify practical solutions that may eradicate fear from your life. Often in life fear is what holds us back from truly fulfilling our dreams. You've probably heard of the famous saying, "Feel the fear and do it anyway."

Fear can be a driving force within you that pushes you forward. Use the fear and work through it to get to the other side of the rainbow, where you will find the pot of gold.

> *"And one day she discovered that she was fierce, and strong, and full of fire, and that not even she could hold herself back because her passion burned brighter than her tears."*
> – Mark Anthony

Chapter 9
Getting On With Life: Special Occasions

Holidays can be a quandary for single parents. And I must say I've not met many parents who delight in taking their children away alone. This I find deeply sad. Over the past few years, holidays alone with my children both at home, abroad and on our camping adventures have been the happiest times of my life.

I know it's scary, it was for me the first time; however, you *must* embrace it with full force. It was the first summer after the split, and my boys and I had endured a horrible few months. I was determined that just because I was on my own, my boys would not miss out on special holidays abroad. We had always had holidays abroad as a family. Why shouldn't we do this because it was just the three of us? For as long as I could sustain the cost, I decided I would do this.

Since the separation, I've been the parent giving my boys holidays, so I have felt a tremendous responsibility to give them the memories of childhood holidays that will reside with them for life. I remember each holiday I took as a child and I believe that you should endeavour to make them as special and as memorable as possible. They're a fantastic opportunity to come together, relax, have fun, and try new experiences as a family.

So, I took the bull by both horns and booked an all-inclusive trip to Kos in Greece for one week. I felt a new sense of responsibility when we arrived at the airport. This was totally down to me. Remembering the passports, discovering where to go, and getting where we needed to be on time and in one piece. It was a test, but the main challenge was not where we went or how to get there. It was with myself and how I felt about the people who judged me and the things I knew I would have to overcome. People gave me a confused and disturbing look.

"Is she on her own with her children?"

"Table for four, Madame?"

"No, there's just the three of us, thank you."

At the bar in the evening, when the kids would be off playing or dipping a toe in the pool, I was sat alone, drink in hand, pretending this was just normal. I didn't know back then, but for me, this would become "my normal." The odd person would say hi or strike up a conversation. But most people don't really want to talk to you, especially if they don't want their husbands talking to you. "That strange woman is on her own with her kids. No one to go on holiday with. How sad!"

But it's not sad at all. I discovered on that holiday that my children and I enjoyed our holidays together far more than we ever did when Dad was around. We had a new sense of freedom and were totally relaxed. We had fun and lots of adventures, so that one holiday was overwhelmingly special. I remember the night before as we were about to leave for home, we were taking our last dusky sunset walk to the restaurant. My boys told me it was the best holiday they had ever been on! I could have burst into tears, but I just hugged them and agreed. Wow, as a "normal" family we had taken them twice to Disneyland Florida. But this was the best one yet?

When I returned home, I remember I felt a new sense of empowerment, a kind I had never felt before. I did it, and it was bloody amazing. We went on trips, walked inside a volcano, had dinner watching the sun go down, and swam after midnight. My eldest did his first paraglide while my youngest was scarred for life, clinging onto me in the speedboat. We laughed and laughed and made memories. Childhood holiday memories.

Perfect. Job done.

Crazy Camping Calamity

Over the next few years, we had many more holidays together. Each one amazing, each one a joy. I would urge any single parent to just do it. And don't just go for the easy option of going with friends and family members. Take the time alone with your children and enjoy all that is awesome about holidays. This is family time.

We have completed trips abroad, weekends away in the UK, Scotland together for the new year. And when money became an issue (due to my rocketing legal costs) we still didn't go without a holiday. I decided (with a little help from my counsellor) to buy a tent. I had always wanted to give them a camping experience, so it made perfect sense and was much more cost effective. It was a huge adventure from the very start. The excitement of going to buy the tent and all the bits and bobs we would need.

I remember our first camping trip. The tent had never been out of the bag along with the cooker, blow-up beds, etc., all still in their boxes. We turned up to our carefully selected camping site in Eskdale in the Lake District, full of hope and excitement in our bellies.

It was Easter, early April, the temperature had dropped spectacularly in the few days before the trip. I didn't have the heart to postpone, despite my better judgement. It was a small authentic site at the foot of Scafell Pike (the highest mountain in England). Absolutely breathtaking scenery with a little snow edge at the peak of the mountain tops.

As we booked in, I remember looking at the site caretaker and telling him it was our first trip. I politely enquired that if I got a bit "lost" with everything, would he be able to help me? He looked at the boys and dog in the car and must have seen the look of sheer terror on my face at the prospect of setting up before darkness set in.

He directed me to a pitch, and I started to unload my packed-to-within-an-inch-of-its-life Toyota Yaris. After five minutes, I looked up and across the field, I saw five strapping men and one lady walk over to us. They were all veterans of camping and an absolute ray of sunshine. "Come on love, we will have this up for you in no time!" And they proceeded to give me and the boys a lesson in all things camping.

That night we all bedded down in our new camping kingdom – me, the boys and the dog. Life was good. Once again, Mummy had done the impossible. I really was here, giving my boys a camping encounter.

When I woke the next morning, it was minus four. Yep...it really was. I'd never been so cold in the night. I was completely covered by my sleeping bag, bar a small hole to breathe. Both the boys were still asleep. I tried to light my new camping fire and set it next to my new carbon monoxide monitor. A very practical safety purchase, so I didn't kill us! You see I had done my research, even though I was catastrophically out of my comfort zone. My main priority was to be safe, have fun, and create memories.

The following year, being truly competent at this camping lark, we went on three camping trips over the summer. The most memorable was at a truly magnificent site called Shell Island, just off the coast of North Wales near Harlech. The site had a causeway access that could only be crossed when the tide was low. Of course, this was extremely exciting. The prospect of being stranded on an island, maybe being captured by pirates or discovering buried treasure. We did have vivid imaginations!

The whole of the island was a campsite, and you could camp anywhere you liked. It was absolutely stunning with outstanding views over the sand dunes, across the huge beach to the Irish Sea. We found a nicely protected and private pitch and set up our magical camping kingdom once again. The magnificent thing about camping is the freedom and safety it gives your children. Not an iPad in sight, no wifi to disrupt the flow of wild happiness and being at one with nature, your bare feet, and the sea. I remember that first evening: We watched the sun go down from the top of a huge sand dune, the boys wild with excitement. A deep warmth of satisfaction and love flowed through my body, like lava spewing from the mouth of a volcano.

This was the holiday where we climbed the highest mountain in Wales, Mount Snowdon. It was an epic walk, the kind we had never tackled before. We walked for as far as we could see, then we walked again as far as we could see. This carried on for hours. I remember coming to a small hut that served drinks and cold snacks, and discovering that this was only the halfway point. *What?!* I tried to play down my fear and trepidation to the boys. My youngest was looking concerned and on the verge of refusing to continue. But together, my boys, the dog, and I put one foot in front of the other, and for four and a half solid hours, we made it to the top.

There are few things in life more satisfying than walking to the top of a mountain. Each time you stop and look back the view gets better and better. It takes your breath away with every gentle turn. It's a magnificent feat, especially for a seven-year-old who had never walked as far in his life. He was so happy with his achievement; I remember when he returned to school in September, he told his teacher he had climbed Mount Everest. It was, however, his Everest, his greatest achievement to date.

Taking on adventures as a family is a great way to really discover our individual strengths and abilities. How we handle difficulties in our adventures helps us to handle difficulties in our lives. In fact, we have this amazing ability as a family now to have the most fun during our periods of adversity. We do this by always finding the humour in every situation.

A great example of this was towards the end of our holiday at Shell Island. It had been a wonderful day; however, an awful storm set in for the evening. A horrendous night ensued, and

I seemed to lay awake for most of it, wondering if the tent was going to take flight. The sounds of the relentless weather plagued the long hours of darkness. I finally managed to get some sleep in the early hours (the boys didn't wake up once).

It was around 7am when I awoke, dreary-eyed, cold and exhausted. I got up from my blow-up bed and put my foot on the hard ground. Except it wasn't hard, it was soft and mushy. I felt around a little further with my foot and knew something was dreadfully wrong. As I squelched to the zipper of the tent I slowly began to realise that the feeling beneath my feet was water – damp waterlogged earth. I put my head through the tiny hole in the door and before me was a sea of about four inches of water. Not just in front of me but for about 300 feet in each direction.

Yes, our lovely tent was now sitting in an immense reservoir of water.

Horrified. That word is just one from a long list of words that I could use to describe my feelings at that moment. I couldn't believe what I saw, *everything* was wet and waterlogged. Our shoes were floating around like boats on a calm sea. The poor dog (a small miniature poodle) couldn't wade through the water, so we picked her up and put her in the car for refuge – the car that was surrounded by water.

I wanted to leave the whole lot, jump in the car and go home to cry. However, my eldest son, with his awe-inspiring resolve, said, "We're not leaving our tent behind, we will pack it all up in the car as best we can, Mum." *And that is what we did.*

We couldn't take everything home, but we got the tent in (without the awning) and most of our important items that were expensive to replace. I started the car with my fingers crossed, and we set off out of the lake around us and headed home. We were so cold and wet, with soggy feet and drenched shoes and clothes. We were extraordinarily hungry, but looking like stowaways, I wasn't sure where we would be able to stop and eat. After about 20 minutes on the road our "Ice Cold In Alex" appeared before us.

(*Ice Cold in Alex* is a compelling film set during World War 2. In North Africa, a medical field unit is forced to cross the desert to reach the British lines in Alexandria. The story focuses on this journey and Captain Anson – played by John Mills – who is tired and thirsty and throughout the film longs for his first ice-cold beer in Alexandria. Let's say he was not disappointed!)

It was a rundown transport café that did the best English Breakfast we had ever tasted. Whilst sat in that cheap café, we saw the extremely funny side of the last few hours. We laughed, joked, and talked over what was to become one of our funniest stories. We still discuss and share this today with each other and anyone else who will listen.

Therefore, in the face of adversity, good things will come. How very true.

Celebrating Mother's and Father's Days

Take a moment here to reflect on your own experiences of these days, before your split. Fun-filled days with breakfast in bed. Maybe you were the one who got longer, lazy time in bed in the morning, while your partner prepared your breakfast. Maybe you got a present or two, or a piece of wonderful and colourful artwork produced by your offspring. Then later in the day maybe a trip to see grandparents as a family unit, coming together to eat, drink and be happy. Truly special days and memories, yes?

These are days that should be filled with love and contentment and are a special family celebration. However, as a divorcing single mum, at best they can be bittersweet. Both have their challenges in slightly different ways. Even weeks before the day, no end of problems can occur. Depending on the relationship you have with your ex, it could be a challenge to even see your child on this memorable day. And let's not forget, this day isn't about Mum or Dad, it's about children learning to appreciate their parents, and to be kind and thankful to them. It is often a great form of excitement for little ones too.

Now if this special day doesn't fall on your designated weekend, or if it's not your week according to your court order, you might find access is denied. Sadly, this happens to countless women and men across the world.

In this area, I consider myself to have been especially lucky, as we always managed to make arrangements to suit these days. Sometimes it was a bit difficult; however, thankfully I have never *not* seen my boys on Mother's Day. And I have always happily returned the favour on Father's Day. I know, I can't believe it either. It's one of those days that if you cause trouble, you should probably expect trouble back in return. And like most things, it's only the children who suffer.

I absolutely love Mother's Day especially when the boys have put a lot of thought and care into the day. I have received poems and been adorned with presents and breakfast in bed. I remember one year there was so much butter on my toast that I thought eating it would cause instant heart failure. But it's not about the taste, it's about their effort. It's about seeing that amazing look of wonder and cleverness in their eyes. "Look what I did for you, Mummy!"

During the early years of singledom, I felt that my boys overcompensated because they could feel and see my pain. They just wanted me to be OK and not feel stressed. Children see more than we give them credit for and as much as you try to hold things back from them, they know when you're really struggling. And there is nothing you or they can do to make it better. It's all part of the process. Again, in this space, it's easy to feel guilty about this, but it's not fruitful to feel this way. This is real life. All you can do through the uncertainty is to ensure that your children feel your undeniable and everlasting love. If they know they will never lose this, it makes all the other "stuff" they must deal with a whole lot easier.

I find Father's Day more emotionally draining, mainly because I lost my dad to cancer just a year before the split. So in the early days, I was extremely raw from that. And on this day, when I was feeling vulnerable, I lost my boys too. They went off to adorn gifts and love on a man who had and was causing me a hefty amount of emotional pain and strife. Perfect, eh? Left alone and depressed once again in my house, mourning my dad and my broken marriage.

I suppose what made these times harder for me was that I had no family support around me. I only really had my mum, who lived in a different county and was not close by to pop in when I needed a hug. Friends are often busy with their own Father's Day plans, so you're left alone and miserable. At times, you muster the strength to be positive, get out, go for a walk, go shopping, and take your mind off things. It works for a short while until you return to your graveyard of a house – silent, cold, lonely.

I'm talking here about the "dark years," the years when the divorce is raging at full throttle. It does get easier. But how long does it take to get to a better place? I can't tell you. I have one friend who had not seen her two children on Mother's Day for five years. Yep, five whole precious years. Despondent and dismissive of it, she has now accepted that it's not going to be an event that she shares with her children until they get much older. Isn't that just totally sad, for her *and* her babies? Divorce is very cruel in many ways, but acceptance can sometimes help to get you through. Some battles you win and others you must let slip away, for your own sanity.

"God, grant me the serenity to accept the things I cannot change, the courage to change the things I can, and the wisdom to know the difference."
– Reinhold Niebuhr

Christmas

Because it was September when the split happened, Christmas was just around the corner. And although I was suffering with devastating heartache and trying to make things work daily, we did feel a sense of relief. The boys and I were happier in the house, and I cherished that new feeling. Christmas however stirs up a multitude of feelings, and I knew getting to the 1st of January was going to be a challenge.

I pushed this fear deep inside and went on to enjoy the new empowerment that came with being totally in control of what we did. In previous years there was always confrontation about buying gifts for the boys, as my ex didn't believe you should spend a lot on your children. He thought that £50 would cover it…when it clearly doesn't. We had the means to give them nice presents, and we both had good full-time jobs. But I had to do my best to make their presents look as big as possible on Christmas morning. This involved buying cheaper toys in large boxes.

Let's face it: Young children just want to see a humongous pile of presents from Santa. And why not? Don't get me wrong; I don't believe you should spoil children and give them everything they desire. But what better feeling than giving your children a wondrous Christmas morning? We'd had lots of disagreements about what I was not allowed to buy for the boys, especially when it came to main presents.

That is why I took this new empowerment to a new level that first year. Yes, looking back, I was compensating for what I knew, deep inside, was probably going to be the most difficult Christmas we had ever been through as a family. And it was; that Christmas was truly the worst in so many ways.

We were in the early days of separation before the divorce lawyers got involved, and before court orders set out access. So we had to piece together the arrangements for the holiday period. Doing this when communication is at a tremendous low takes time and patience. Eventually, we decided that I would have the boys Christmas Eve, and they would go to my ex's at 2pm on Christmas Day. That's OK I thought, Christmas Eve had, for years, always been a day that I had spent with the boys. And it was – still is – very special to us. And obviously, I could have the Christmas morning I had wanted to have for many years.

You see, as a child, I would rip open my presents with pure excitement and glee. However, my ex only allowed them to open three or four small presents when they woke up. Then they would have to wait until his family had arrived and everyone would open presents together, one by one. Sort of kills the childlike excitement of Christmas morning. Having to watch Nana open a scented candle before you could dive into your next toy.

The build-up to Christmas was great fun for me and the boys. I had always loathed having a real tree that was a nightmare after a week when all the needles seemed to drop off speedily and stick to your feet. This year, we went shopping for a new tree. We chose a stunner – beautiful shades of white with glorious decorations. It was luxurious and spectacular. We decorated it, listening to Christmas music, and dancing around the living room, me with a glass of mulled wine and the boys eating mince pies. We still have the tree, as it's become a symbol of freedom to me now.

My mum, who sometimes came for Christmas, had decided this year to spend the holidays with my sister in Yorkshire. I had been estranged from my sister for several years, so I was a little disappointed that my mum wouldn't be with us at this difficult time. I kept this from her, however, and pretended that it was OK. I told her that Sarah, my good friend, had invited me for dinner and not to worry; I would be fine. I don't think I ever really believed this, but I was kidding her and myself. Sarah had very kindly invited me to have Christmas dinner with her and her family after 2pm. She is such a special soul and a great friend, and she knew I would find Christmas Day hard, probably more than I did. So that was all sorted. We would have a wonderful Christmas morning; the boys would go at 2pm, and then I would have a glorious meal with a great friend and her family. The best of both worlds! Perfect.

On Christmas morning, there was a mass of toys in the living room, and the boys and I woke early to get started on the excitement of ripping and being able to open all our presents with no delays! Absolute bliss! Yes?

No.

In reality, it was a disaster. I had fantasised about having a perfect Christmas morning. But I didn't factor in how I would feel, and how the boys would feel given the fact that this was our first Christmas as a "broken" family. I was tense, the boys were strained. They easily became annoyed when I couldn't put their toys together or even just get them out of the box. Why do companies package toys in boxes, where you need a sledgehammer to get them out (or a screwdriver at least)?

At the back of all our minds was the fact that we had to do this quickly, as 2pm was looming and we would have to part. Although we were up at around 6am, the shorthand moved around the clock face with surprising speed that morning.

I had bought my eldest a basketball net, but he struggled to put it together and as I'm useless at putting anything together, we didn't actually get it set up. He was disappointed, I was frustrated, and the morning came crashing down around us. No amount of presents or Christmas cheer could take away the pain we all felt inside on this day. Of course, the boys wanted to leisurely play with their new toys, but then I had to usher them to the bathroom and get ready to go. Since it was agreed, I had been secretly dreading 2pm on Christmas Day. Now it had become a reality.

There was a knock at the door. The boys gave me a kiss and, with a sad look in their eyes and probably a feeling of guilt for leaving me, they went. I closed the door. I was alone in my house of horror again. I turned, walked to the fridge, picked up a bottle of white wine and a full box of Milk Tray chocolates, and made my way upstairs. I sent Sarah a quick apology text, saying I just couldn't go for Christmas dinner. I collapsed in a heap on my bed and wailed and balled in a fit of uncontrollable crying. I felt like my insides had been ripped from me. I have never felt such hurt, like I was slowly dying inside. I drank the bottle of wine, ate all the chocolates and passed out, heartbroken.

I slept for hours, as it was mid-evening when I woke. I only remember walking back downstairs, getting another bottle of wine, and going back to bed.

The next day, I was still in bed when I heard a knock at the door. It was around lunchtime. I walked downstairs to try to see who it was, as I was surely not going to open the door to anyone. Through the small gap in the shutters, I saw Sarah, holding a covered plate. I opened the door and she said, "You couldn't come for Christmas dinner, so I've brought Christmas dinner to you." The kind amazing soul that she is, she had reserved one extra plate and brought it around for me. How amazingly wonderful. She could see from my teary face that I was in no way able to even talk to her, so she handed it over and said she was there for me when I needed her.

With tears now rolling down my face I heated my Christmas dinner in the microwave. It was gorgeous, cooked to perfection with all the trimmings, and it was probably the best Christmas meal I have ever had. Each mouthful was filled with love and compassion.

There you have it. My all-time Christmas low.

Since then, on Christmas Day, I have been thankful for all the good things in my life. I remember 2pm that awful Christmas day, and am grateful for how far we have come as a family. I thank the Lord that things will never get as bad as they did that day. Little did I know at the time, however, that I would spend the next five years fighting and enduring more trauma and pain. The following year, when we were negotiating what was to become the terms of the court order or access arrangements, to my complete surprise, my ex didn't want to have any access on Christmas day. I was super happy about this as I didn't want to go through the same as the previous year. He was happy to have them on Boxing Day instead. Of course, I knew that this was so that he could go out and get drunk on Christmas Eve, and have an "adult" Christmas Day. I knew that was more appealing to him. At the same time, I also found it very sad for the boys; however, they were much happier knowing that we had the whole day together. In fact, in their eyes, they got two Christmas days. And what child wouldn't like that?

When you're considering your parent plan, it's easy to overlook significant days like Christmas. I urge you to think hard about the options available to you when negotiating crucial and momentous days. When you're in the courthouse, you may not care too deeply about these days, as your foremost thinking is about the everyday weekly schedule. But believe me, if you're not happy with the agreements for these days it's much harder to change it once the plan is written down in black and white on court paper. In fact, any future changes you want to make *will* be extremely costly. More than the cost of a nice holiday for you and your children!

Ensure you have a few options and suggestions to start the negotiations. Almost every little detail may need some form of consultation, depending on how awkward your ex is likely to be. You have to consider that you may need to change the way you've experienced these days previously. If this is the case, consider what changes will bring new happiness and joy. How can you incorporate new traditions into these days? The lives of everyone concerned are going through massive change. Look for positive alternatives for your new life, especially for family occasions.

The Dreaded School Play

Of course, we love to see our little ones at Harvest Festivals, singing with their little classmates songs they've been learning for many weeks. And Christmas wouldn't be Christmas without the wonderful School Play, which I hasten to add, rarely features baby Jesus these days. There are two sides to all of this as you navigate divorce and the years that follow while your children are at "little" school. The wonderment of moments is captured on video, as your little one notices where you are sat in the audience, and gives you a huge wave and warm smile.

Then there is your other side. The dark side. Somewhere in the audience is your ex and his mother-in-law, or heaven forbid their new girlfriend. Luckily, I never had to deal with a new partner at these events, but I know many who have. Attending these proceedings alone is at best traumatic, as you try to balance the emotion of watching your child sing and the nervousness of locking eyes with someone you truly can't stand. Coming face to face with someone who is causing you so much pain and angst is overwhelmingly difficult, especially when you're in the company of so many other couples. Yes, the parents are still together as a "whole" family, chatting away with what you see as them rubbing their faces in your misery. The number of times I've had to dig deep and hold back the tears is substantial. In fact, every event I went to has been extremely hard for me. These were the first five years after my breakup, and as you know by now, they were an emotional rollercoaster.

I am thankful, however, that I had another child to take with me, so I wasn't sat on my own waiting for the curtain to go up. I always ensured I arrived very early to get a good seat near the front. Then the horrendous 45-minute wait while other parents arrived, knowing that at some point "he" was going to walk in. He was always late, so I knew that he would be standing at the back. I could always feel his eyes burning into the back of my head.

If I hadn't noticed him for fear of turning around and locking eyes, by the time my child came onto the stage I would see him waving at me, and then waving at his dad. This broke my heart. I could see how awkward it was for him too. Displaying the same attention to both of us, in different locations around the school hall. Afterwards, the children would collect their things while the parents patiently waited. Which parent does your child go to first? What an awful decision for any child. This often depended on whose "night" it was – who he was going home with. Of course, I always wanted him to come home with me, especially after a big night of performance. However, sometimes I had just a minute or so to tell him how amazing he was and then watched him go over to his dad and walk away.

Nobody tells you when you get divorced that there will be so many different challenges to face. Parenting through divorce and afterwards is heartbreaking, challenging, and exhausting. I do believe the only thing that got me through these events was wine. Yes, I know, how very sad. But I always ensured there was a bottle of wine in the fridge to calm the nerves and tension and to help me sleep after the trauma of school plays.

The most testing school event I experienced, without a doubt, was my eldest's leaving assembly. It was just a few months after the split when he was leaving "small" school to move on to "big" school. This is a monumental step for any parent, especially for your first child. Your child is growing up, he's not a tiny tot anymore, and he's venturing onto new pastures after seven years in the same school. This was a daytime event, so I had to go it alone. However, as this was my eldest and my ex had completely cut him out of his life at this point, my son only had *me* there. He would become very familiar with this feeling, but it crucified me that after nine years of having a father, that man didn't care about him at all. He was only concerned with the child who was of his blood. I was broken before the event even started and holding back the tears.

This was a celebration of their junior years in school, with songs to be sung and photographs taken over the years exhibited on a big screen. Even now as I write, I get emotional thinking about sitting there in total distress, pushing the intensity of my despair away while trying to smile at my boy as he sang. Afterwards, I said my goodbyes to him and how proud I was and almost ran to the car. I just about made it when my tears fell like waterfalls. Luckily, I was parked on a quiet street as I gushed and cried. I was numb driving home. I had been numb for a long time. I felt hopeless, I wanted the divorce to be over. Little did I know that it would take many more years for it to be over.

While we are on the subject of school, there is another challenging aspect to manoeuvre through: the dreaded Parents' Evenings. In the days and hours leading up to these, I felt myself becoming very anxious. I knew I had to get through about 20 minutes sat side by side with *him* in front of the teacher, trying to hide the catastrophe of our relationship. Looking back, I don't think we achieved this, and I do sympathise with the many teachers who are confronted by two divorcing parents. I know people who refuse to do this and have separate meetings. Unfortunately, this wasn't an option at my school, so it had to be done. Thirty minutes, and I would be back home being comforted by my trusted bottle of wine. I can do this.

I will admit to being very angry at some points, especially in the early days. That anger was fuelled by the actions of my ex, and his sheer resistance to make this an easier process. In fact, I knew that his mission in the early years was to make my life a living hell. And he achieved that stupendously. During the meeting with the teacher, we would be calm and gracious, and crack the odd joke. He would flash his eyes at the teacher in his bid for her to think he was such a wonderful man and a fantastic loving father. This irritated the hell out of me because he was none of those things. He expertly reflected his true narcissistic tendencies – those same tendencies that drew me to him years before. But I know the real man. I knew he didn't bother to read every night. I know he was *only* out for himself and didn't care about the fragile hearts and minds of my children. I now know that he must have received great delight from my frustration. He wanted to see me angry, hurt and broken.

By the time my youngest was at "big" school, we had managed to get through the desperate first five years of divorce and I had done a lot of work on myself and my reactions. He was no longer important in my life and that's how I treated him – with minimal contact and matter-of-fact behaviour. I would not let him see me broken. I had learnt to be strong by now. Of course, he still played the concerned loving father trying to win over the teachers. But I didn't let it affect me. Also, at senior school you attend with your child, so all three of us would rock up together and spend at least two hours going from one teacher to another. You see he was never really that interested in education, or any significant parenting for that matter. He just had visitation rights and would see his son but never actually get involved or have the conversations needed.

So, what advice can I give you? Well, I would say try to not let your feelings get the better of you when in the company of your ex in these situations. I wasn't very good at this initially. Try to remember that this is also extremely difficult for your child. Some parents manage to present a united front when with their children, and I certainly commend them for that. However, don't beat yourself up if this is as impossible as it was for me. Oh, and always keep a bottle of wine in the fridge for special occasions. Sometimes the special occasion is that you've got a bottle of wine in the fridge. Remember, anybody who is trying to bring you down is already beneath you.

Chapter 10
Getting On With Life:
The Day to Day

Most people go through life with little or no understanding of the impact that divorce has on those who experience this life-changing event.

I remember one day at work, I sat next to my boss, who had been happily married for around eight years and had two gorgeous children. His wife was away for the weekend on a work trip. It was a Friday afternoon and he turned to me and said, "Oh Ang, I've got the kids all weekend as my wife is away, so it's going to be a hard weekend. I'm probably going to be late on Monday too as I've got to get them ready for school. What a nightmare."

He was bracing himself for a busy tiring weekend. I paused for a moment and looked at him, and at that moment he realised, "Oh yes, you do this every weekend don't you?" I smiled and said, "Yes, that is my everyday. I do everything for my two boys alone with no help." We laughed and I think he felt quite embarrassed, but at that moment he had an epiphany. He had a lightbulb moment about what my life was like as a full-time mum, with a full-time stressful job, and no help.

Divorce impacts just about every part of your life – from childcare to moving house. Weddings and family gatherings hold newfound issues to deal with. Those odd jobs around the house all of a sudden become your responsibility. Here I give some insight into the everyday nuances of being a divorced single parent.

Childcare

It can be difficult to juggle the demands of childcare with two parents. However, the challenges of this as a single parent alongside holding down full-time or even part-time employment are testing at best. You want the very best care for your children, but you also need to balance that against convenience, availability and affordability.

In the months leading up to my initial separation, I knew that I needed a different job with working hours that would be more manageable for school drop-off and pick-up times. I also wanted to "be there" as much as possible after school. These were turbulent times, and the last thing I wanted was to be getting home after 6pm when bedtime shortly followed. My children needed me to be there for them as much as possible, but I also needed to work full time. I found a job working a permanent 8am to 4pm shift, which was the best option at that time.

Before the divorce, my ex had a very flexible job and did most of the school pick-ups. After we split, he would only pick the children up on their allocated nights with him. He wouldn't even help until I had childcare figured out. As he said many times, "If I'm picking them up from school, they will stay with me that night." Of course, he did this to make my life as difficult as possible, knowing that it was impossible for me to get to school at 3:30pm.

I used various childcare methods at this time, usually making me late for work in the morning and a mad scramble to a childminder after work. Being late consistently was stressful and unsustainable. However, picking your children up from a childminder who clearly wasn't invested in the wellbeing of your child was tough, especially when there didn't seem to be any other options available to me. The evenings grew darker in the winter months and the early evening sky was pitch black by 5pm. I knew in the minds of my boys it felt like 8pm some days, as they patiently waited for me. I would be overcome with frequent feelings of guilt as I looked into their eyes.

After struggling for a number of months and having exhausted the local childminders who collected from my school, I was at my wit's end. No employer wants to hear that you're finding it hard to even get to work on time. And I would fly out of work as the clock struck four to get back as soon as possible. I decided that I needed to fix this problem once and for all, and proceeded to look for someone who could help me with this conundrum. I was hesitant at first, but put an advertisement on an online childcare website anyway. I needed someone to come to the house no later than 7:15 in the morning so I could get to work on time without breaking the speed limit. I needed them to walk my boys to school but then come back at 3:30pm and take my boys home until I got back from work. I knew that was a tall order.

To this day I still refer to Julia as an angel sent from above. She was from Romania and in her early 20s. She lived with her boyfriend who was studying at Manchester University. I will never forget the day she first came to the house for an interview. She was like a beautiful shining light with an engaging smile and calm demeanour. The boys loved her immediately, as did I. Bless her, she would come to my house in the wet, dark and cold winter mornings and lovingly take my fragile boys into her care. When I returned home around 4:30pm, she was playing and laughing with them. It's a strange and uncomfortable feeling to leave your most precious babies with a stranger. It was a leap of faith indeed, but she was a miracle who came to help me when nobody else could.

Many people rely on family to help with childcare. However, I had no family living nearby. I only had my mother, who lived an hour's drive away so she was never on hand to help. Most of the time I felt as though I had the whole world on my shoulders. Julia spoke good but broken English. We never discussed my situation, but I know she knew that she was much more to me than childcare. She gave me the wonderful gift of knowing my children were safe and happy. And she knew they needed more than just her practical help. They needed safety and gentle kindness, which she provided in bucket loads. If this book is ever published, I will send her a copy and hope she can read about the immense impact she had on me and my boys. Due to the wonderful world of Facebook, I know that she has returned to Romania, married her boyfriend and now has two beautiful twin daughters. Thank you, Julia, my angel sent from above.

Childcare can be one of the most arduous problems to resolve. It can weigh heavy on you and cause a remarkable amount of Mum Guilt! We're talking about who you trust with your little ones. Is there anything more challenging than getting this right? Because if you don't get it right your children will suffer.

There are many different options and wouldn't it be amazing if we could all employ Mary Poppins to save us and sprinkle a spoonful of sugar on our daily lives? My advice is to do as much due diligence as you can to feel comfortable. Just like in the solicitor's office that time when I failed to ask questions! Asking as many questions as possible will help with this process. I will say that again as it's super important: *Ask questions.* Get to know the person you're entrusting with the lives of your children. Write down at least 10 questions you *need* to ask when interviewing hired help or speaking to child care providers.

It's also important to provide clear guidelines about your expectations, and in particular, be unambiguous about *what you don't want*. What rules do you have for your children that you expect to be adhered to? Do all of the above and then trust your gut! If your gut is telling you something is off, listen to it. It could have been the best interview or conversation but if you don't get the "feeling" this is your person – your children's person – walk away and find someone else. In the same manner, if your children are not happy following a session of childcare, change it. When you pick them up they should be full of smiles, joy and excitement to see you. If they are quiet and sad with low energy then you need to make a change immediately. Find your Julia!

Moving House

Another aspect of divorce that I certainly didn't consider initially is moving houses. At first, I was intent on the possibility of staying in the family home, as I thought it would be the best option for my boys. They were experiencing enough upheaval, and I knew that the whole prospect of moving to a new house and turning their lives upside down *again* would have a detrimental effect on their well-being. Home was what they were familiar with, their safe place, and it was where we were learning to live together as a unit of three. It was where their memories resided, their ultimate hobbit hole.

However, as I was slowly realising that my ex was working to make my life as difficult as possible, he forced me into a situation where the only option was to sell the house. So, it had to be done and was the next huge step we all had to endure. Yes, divorce and moving to a new house are two of the most stressful life events you can go through. However, you must find the strength to endure both at the same time.

With no other option for our home, the haven that my boys and I had cultivated was on the open market to the highest bidder. How was I going to get through this emotionally and practically?

Fact is, I moved to a new house twice in six months alone, with a 6- and a 10-year-old. With no family help, just my boys and me. Oh yes, and a good few bottles of wine!

The house sold in the first two days of being advertised. This spun me into a frenzy of what needed to be done. Sorting out cupboards, clearing rooms alongside endless trips to the tip at the weekend. I was overwhelmed by the work involved. Clearing out the garden shed and the rubbish in the attic, and of course with no help at all from my ex. I had made my bed and he was making me lie in it.

In the first few weeks, I decided to try to sell the things we had no use for at various car boot sales. Early one Sunday morning we all woke at 5am (yes on a Sunday!), packed the car full of our unwanted goods and set off. Arriving shortly after 6am we were excited to "play shop" for the morning. We displayed all our items around the car boot and on an old wallpaper table. It was fun. Well, we made it fun. We made about £80 for a morning's work and returned home after a well-deserved trip to McDonald's for a Happy Meal.

After another couple of weeks, we returned but made only £15 this time for all that hard work. It was a different feeling this time with a different clientele. Most people wanted to pay pennies and would offer ridiculous amounts for our precious belongings. They were like vultures preying on our story of woe. I decided that this was the last car boot sale we would go to. Some items we took to the charity shop, but due to the speed of the sale, the last few weeks were frantic. We made countless trips to the tip to get ready to move.

Financially, we had not resolved the legal agreement as part of the divorce, and due to the speed of the sale, I was forced to look for rented accommodation. Time was running out, all the houses we had viewed so far were atrocious. How could I move my boys to a smelly, dirty lifeless place? One day we looked around a small but delightful two-bedroom cottage. Yes, it was small, but I knew we could be happy moving there. I was desperate at this point and pleaded with the old lady to let me have it. She was rather taken with my boys and could see the desperation on my face. At last, we had somewhere to call home.

Moving day came upon me so quickly. I remember on the morning of the move I still had many boxes to pack. My wardrobe was still untouched. As the removal men arrived, I remember desperately throwing clothes still on hangers into boxes. My eldest son was amazing. I had kept him off school to help with the move. He was only 10, but he was extremely practical and strong.

Two more angels came to me that day: the kindest removal men on the planet. Once they realised I was alone with my boy, facing the monumental and challenging task of moving home they tenderly tried to wash my stress away and went above and beyond. "It's no problem, love, we will get it all done, don't worry," they said to me. They were amazed that my son was so helpful too and recognised that he was trying to help his mum, who had been through a significant period of pain.

The strain of the previous day was in my eyes: the day of my first court appearance for the divorce. We had waited such a long time for a date, to ask for it to be changed would have caused a further significant delay. So, I had no option and no time to absorb the anguish of that initial day in court, before I was flung into the upheaval of moving home. I really don't know how I managed, however you just do. You must.

I had to put some of our things into storage as they wouldn't fit in the small two-bedroom cottage. I bought bunk beds that my 10-year-old spent a day erecting. I was never any good with flat-packed furniture. Thank goodness my son was able to despite his young years. Six months later we did it all again, into a bigger rental so that I no longer had to pay a significant amount for storage. The financial aspect of my divorce continued to be unresolved, but I found a new home that we were all immensely excited about. The boys had a bedroom each again and we could build our new haven: a place to rest our heads, feel safe and enjoy being together again. We stayed in this home for many years, not wanting to uproot my boys again and not financially being able to buy a house once the particulars of finances had been resolved.

Finding a new place to call home was a good turning point. I know I reluctantly left the marital home. That said, our new place no longer had the bad memories that were embedded in the walls. There was no reminder of their father there, it was our place and our place alone. In hindsight, I do think it made a massive difference to me, living in a home different from where I was married. It was a fresh start. A new beginning. A new method of surviving this journey of life and divorce.

Weddings, Birthdays and Family Do's

It's a strange feeling, having lived through years of going to events, weddings, funerals, engagements, etc. together or as a family. That all changes with divorce.

In the first few years, everyone notices the fact that you're not together with your ex. As years go by people wonder why you're still single. Why can't she find a man? What's wrong with her? To this day, having spent over 12 years as a single mum, I still dread the incoming invitations. I know I should see them as gifts, a chance to join in whatever celebration is taking place. However, all I see is the embarrassment of being alone and people taking pity on me as I latch onto friends and their partners.

Events where the boys are invited are easier, especially in the early days when your attention is focused on them and you still feel like a family unit. However, events where I tag along with friends so I don't have to walk in alone are awful to endure. As my children got older, they would go off and play and leave me. Of course, I didn't mind as they had friends to play with. And who wants to spend the night with the boring adults? I would ask my eldest not to leave me alone for at least 10 minutes until I had found my feet, or until I had struck up a conversation and felt more comfortable. I would consider myself to be a confident person, however, these situations made me feel so weak, lonely, and fragile.

As the years went on, I had friends who had divorced and married again and separated again, all during the time I was single. Most people had a number two to accompany them more often than not. If possible, I would try to make my excuses. But some events you just need to suck it up and get out there. Not going would be rude and cause offence.

The most significant event I remember was an 18th birthday party for a close friend of my eldest son. I had known him and his family since the boys were five years old, and he was the first of my son's friends to turn 18, a significant milestone in life. It was a lovely event in a beautiful room decorated with pictures to remember and celebrate his 18 years on the planet. He too had divorced parents who were now happily married again. He had a large family and many friends there. I knew a lot of them through our years together at school. I was with friends, it was a happy occasion.

But the truth was, I was dying inside. I felt an immense sadness. I was once again here alone, and feeling alone amongst great friends. How is that even possible? But I assure you it is. As I had become accustomed to, I was holding back the emotion and trying to hide the sadness in my eyes. I remember going to the toilet towards the end of the evening and bursting into tears. Why was I still alone? Why could I not find my happily ever after? Why was life and relationships in general always such a struggle?

A few months after this event, I was talking to my eldest about it. I opened up about how I found the night emotionally traumatic, but I hid my feelings away. Unbelievably he then told me that he felt the same way. He too had spent time outside crying. He didn't have a large family to make an event like this possible and he didn't have a Dad that even knew or cared where he was. His 18th birthday was looming, and his experience would be very different. You see for birthdays and Christmas he only really received presents from me and my mum. No other close or extended family to make a fuss of him. Both his biological father and his father of nine years walked away from him, leaving him shattered. This was a pain I could not carry for him or eradicate for him. And that killed me.

So many good women sleep alone because they know the value of the space beside them. So many good women attend functions alone because they won't accept someone who isn't right for them. The next time you're at a function and you see someone going it alone, make the effort to engage with them and help them feel comfortable and valued. Single isn't a status. It's a word that describes a person who is strong enough to enjoy life without depending on the wrong people.

I Can't Play Football and Sex Education

Growing up I would have considered myself a "girly girl." I was no tomboy and liked all things feminine. Then I gave birth to two boys – my gorgeous boys who are my absolute world. Then I became a single parent of these two boys.

You often hear single mums say, "You must be both Mum and Dad as a single parent." This very much depends on how involved your ex is in your children's lives. In my experience, when the boys did see their dad it was more visitation than parenting. It's usually (but not always) the Mum who does everything for the children, and covers all bases needed.

My ex didn't play with the boys much even when we were together. They didn't go to the park to kick a football around very often at all. As a new single parent, you must now dive headfirst into all the things both mums and dads naturally do.

I was hopeless at football, but having two boys made me learn to appreciate the masculine side of my personality. I didn't really understand "toilet humour"; that said, boys find farts, poops and burps immensely amusing. A mother of boys needs to accept these things as part of normal life, whereas girls will sit quietly and do some colouring or paint a picture.

Boys want to be out and about, getting dirty in the mud and having sword fights. I learnt to embrace all the things that boys love and gradually became more of a tomboy over the years. I'm sure dads of only girls go through the same, learning to appreciate Disney Princess movies and all things pink!

Playing monsters in the forest is one thing, but there are also the more important aspects of life you need to help your children with. Like sex. I had always been very candid with the boys. If they asked a question I would, within reason, answer it. I knew parents who would swerve difficult questions, but fundamentally I knew this was wrong. I clearly remember when my eldest was about five years old, not long after starting school. One evening he asked me, "Mummy what does 'gay' mean?" I explained that it was when two men or two women had a relationship and lived like me and Daddy live. His eyes widened as he realised what I was saying. He thought for a while and just simply said, "Oh, OK then." From that day on, a gay relationship was just normal in his eyes, which is how it should be. There should be no difference in understanding, and by *not* telling your children about these types of things until they get older, *you* make it different.

I adopted the same candid approach to sex. I remember getting a letter from the school detailing that they were about to cover some aspects of sex education. This was when my eldest was still quite young, and I was still married. My ex didn't feel comfortable having any conversations like this and was happy to leave it in the hands of the school. But I wanted my children to hear this from me. I didn't want a stranger to do this, as a parent I felt it was my responsibility. So, I knew this aspect of parenting, like many others, was down to me.

Walking is a great activity to have deep and meaningful conversations. Over the years, my boys and I became adventurous walkers and had some fantastic conversations while doing so.

To discuss the topic of sex with my eldest, I decided to take him out for a walk after school, just the two of us. On this short walk around a local golf course, I effortlessly struck up The Conversation. This led to a few questions, but was, in fact, a really great experience. I believe that doing this early with your children and opening a safe environment to talk is imperative to a long-lasting open relationship. Over the years, the boys grew to know that they could ask me anything.

A tip I received from a friend was to buy a book that detailed everything that a child would need to know concerning sex education. I bought a book called *Where Do Babies Come From*, which is specially written for children with pictures and diagrams to help them understand the basics. This was a lifesaver and helped me to offer explanations. I purposely left this book in their bedrooms also so they could look at it themselves. I knew I didn't want them to learn this stuff from friends or via the internet. Another advantage to doing this yourself is that, following lessons in school about such things, they will feel comfortable asking you any questions they dare not ask in front of their friends.

How Do I Fix That? Odd Job Nightmares

I of course believe in feminism and the empowerment of women; however, I also believe that some jobs are more suited to men or women. I call them "blue jobs" and "pink jobs." Naturally, in most relationships, the men will primarily do certain tasks and the women others. For instance, men traditionally take the bins out, wash the car, fix things, change the lightbulbs. Women tend to do most of the cleaning tasks, change the beds, cook, choose soft furnishings.

At times I found dealing with household jobs as a single mum incredibly stressful. Firstly, you must do everything. That's fine because you just get on with it and do everything. Some women do everything anyway even if a man is living in the house. However, now and again something crops up and you're stuck. You have no idea how to bleed the radiators or work a drill. How do you hang a painting on a wall so it's not wonky? I had no idea how to do many household tasks, especially in the early years. My stress levels were already on high alert due to the divorce, so the frustration of these tasks was overwhelming. I cried at times in these situations as I felt useless and powerless.

I eventually managed to find a good handyman and I would create a list of jobs for his next visit. This obviously costs money, but with no dad or brother to help, I was lost. But I would never be beaten. I think I was lucky in some ways that I rented my house for many years. If anything significant needed doing, it was my landlord's responsibility to fix it. Whew! I was also lucky in the fact that, as my eldest grew, he became incredibly handy. He would delight in helping me and became my "free of charge" handyman. He erected flat-packed furniture in super-quick time while I was still deciding which piece was which. I have always been very careful to not depend on him too much, especially when he was younger. I know after parents separate, boys can take on the extra responsibility of being the "man around the house." And you must try to avoid that if you can – it's too much pressure for a child! However, working as a team and helping each other out is a perfect scenario. They learn and you learn together.

Leaving Your Kids Home Alone

Going out without my children wasn't possible for me for many years. Occasionally friends would help, but you really don't like to ask them frequently. I know most people get a weekend off while their children visit the other parent. I never got this time as I had my eldest every day and every weekend. Which was fine, it was just the way it was. But it did mean that the social aspect of life becomes a challenge. My mum would sometimes come over to babysit, but this didn't happen often as she lived so far away.

I remember one Christmas, I didn't go anywhere at all. I didn't set foot in a bar throughout the whole festive period. As for dating, well, it was practically impossible. Every so often I would try to get a babysitter for an internet first date. Usually, these were terrible, and we'd have two drinks before I would make my excuses. Paying a babysitter makes these useless nights out very expensive indeed.

One day I was visiting one of my good "Divorce Club" friends. We would talk about our experiences and, to each other, became a shoulder to cry on and a sounding board for all things ex-related. I was relaying to her my issues with not getting out. It was summertime and my eldest was around thirteen at this point. I was saying that I couldn't leave him on his own and how difficult it was. She just turned to me and said, "Why can't you leave him?" I thought for a while and said, "Well I've never left him before, and it wouldn't be right." She quite rightly pointed out that it didn't get dark until after 9 or even 10pm. She said I could go out early evening, not too far away and be on the end of the phone. I needed to take baby steps, but he would be perfectly okay in the house in the daylight.

This gave me a lot to think about. Could I do this? I recall Googling at what age you could legally leave your children alone in the house. Surprisingly, there was nothing official and everything I was reading was all about how mature the child was and to do it when it felt right and safe. Well, this was a game-changer for me. I could allow myself to do this and my boy would be OK? Sometimes we need a friend to show us a different aspect of our issues, to tell us it's okay to do something, and make us see our situation with new eyes.

My son was, of course, delighted, and said it was a great idea. "I don't know what you're worrying about, Mum. I will be fine." He liked the new responsibility of being at home alone. Maybe it made him feel like he was older and no longer a small child who needed supervision.

It is a challenge for every parent, whether single or as a couple, and the only advice I can give you is it needs to feel right. Obviously, you can't do it when they're still too young. Around 13 or 14 years old is probably a good time to start leaving them in daylight hours. That's exactly what I did. I would go out for a couple of hours in the afternoon. Then a couple of hours in the early evening, while it was still light. He would always tell me I could stay out longer, but I needed to take it slow.

Dating became possible again, though I never really had much luck in that department. I could meet friends and open a little bit of "me" time. After being totally confined to my home unless I had a babysitter, this gave me a little bit of freedom.

If you feel stuck with little time to yourself, consider what options are available to you. I know, you might not think it's possible, but many times we don't see our own situations clearly. It takes someone else – a friend, family member or counsellor – to make us see things from a different perspective. Take a few days to consider this question, speak to people, get advice from others, and speak to your Divorce Club friends. What do they do differently from you? Can you help each other with childcare so that you both get a break? Keep on pondering this until you have answers. Dare to think and do differently. If you always do what you've always done, you'll always get what you've always got!

Take Pictures and Make Memories, But Be Present

What's an unforgettable gift you can give to your children?

Your time.

Time is the most precious and valuable commodity we own and have 100% control over. We alone can choose how to spend our time, who to spend it with and who *not* to spend it with. Children need plenty of your time, that's never in dispute. But what children really need is dedicated time just for them. They need to see you investing your time in them, and not trying to do a thousand different things at the same time.

We live in a world of crazy busyness, and frequently I see parents constantly multitasking. There is never time devoted to just being together. Parents go to the park with their children and spend the whole of their time on the phone. This breaks my heart. You can see children craving the time of their parents and never really getting a look in. This also breaks my heart.

Take time to just be with your children with no distractions. I know it's not possible 100% of the time, but if you try to build this into your day, your week, or your month, the benefits are amazing. Get on the floor and play, read them a book without skipping any pages (yes, I've been guilty of that one many times). That said, I am not able to write these words because I am perfect. Far from it. I can write these words because I too have faced the same challenges and realised that my children need more of *me*. They don't need fancy clothes or hundreds of pounds spent on them for birthdays and Christmas.

The best gift you can give your children is your time. So, plan this in if it doesn't come naturally. Take some time out to evaluate how much quality time you spend with your children with absolutely no distractions. Develop some rules that will allow you to be with them in the moment. This is a good exercise to include your children in. Ask them what they would like you to do differently. You're not a mind reader, and their answers may surprise you. My youngest absolutely detests me going onto my phone when we're watching a movie. He wants to watch the movie with me fully attentive, not messaging someone from work or a friend. Yes, at times this does drive me mad a little when I need to send someone a quick message. But when he presses the pause button on the remote, it's a gentle reminder to me that time is *the* most important and treasured gift we must give our children.

When reading them a story, how often do our minds wander off to an e-mail we need to send? Or to something we need to purchase on Amazon before the day is done? Of course, there are times when your children need to just understand that you're busy. But if you ensure you make quality time for them too, they will be more understanding of the pressures of life that you can't ignore.

As single parents, we are prone to many different challenges that most families will never be able to fully comprehend. However, on the subject of time, we do have a distinct advantage. Being a single parent affords you more time with your children alone. And this is truly a gift. As a single parent, we have fewer distractions and can devote most, if not all, our time to our children. I know without any doubt that if I hadn't been a single parent I absolutely wouldn't be as close to my children as I am now. And this closeness I do feel will last a lifetime. It is a wonderful foundation for a lifelong amazing relationship with your children.

You have a choice here: to focus on your loneliness and not having a partner to share the ups and downs of life with, or you can focus on your children, in the moments of joy that they bring. The "moment" is where life should be lived. You can create special amazing memories with your children if you use your time well.

Chapter 11
The World of Dating

"The biggest coward of a man is to awaken the love of a woman without the intention of loving her."
– Bob Marley

So I had been through the most terrible few years at the hands of my ex-husband. My eldest son's dad was also a complete nightmare. Both men I'd had children with were *not* what I had dreamt of when I was a little girl.

But good men are out there aren't they? Luckily, I do know some great men who were either married or partnered with friends. They were fantastic fathers. I could not let my experiences cloud my thoughts about men for my future. I had to believe that there was a great man out there for me. Sometimes the love of your life comes after the biggest mistake of your life.

At the time of writing this I am still waiting, even after all these years of being single. I do still believe that one day I will meet a good man to spend the rest of my life with. I also want to be married again, despite what I've been through. But I would never do this unless I was 100% certain, and after a significant time together had elapsed.

So, my outlook has not been tarnished by my experiences of men to date. But how do you go about finding them? Where do you start? How do you know you're ready? What are the rules of dating now? I had no idea. But I did know that I would not find him if I wasn't looking for him. Yes, I'm still looking, but now I accept that this will happen at the right time for me, and I don't believe the right time has come around yet. You need to be with someone who will take care of you. Not in the material sense, but in the sense that he will take care of your soul, your well-being and your heart. You shouldn't give up on men, you should give up on arseholes. Never settle for shitty coffee, shitty friends or shitty men.

You must keep the faith and keep looking. The time to do this is now. Not in 2 years, 5 years or 10 years. I can't stress enough how important it is to try to not let your past experiences spoil your chances of happiness and togetherness with a man who truly deserves you. Remember your power; you are different now. You have the scars of a failed marriage and it has changed you. Many times, I see people rush into another long-term relationship just because they can't bear to be alone. You don't find your worth in a man. You find your worth within yourself and *then* find a man who's worthy of you. Remember that. Don't change yourself so that other people will like you. Be yourself so that the right people will love you. You might know what you want, but more importantly, now you know what you don't want and what you don't deserve. Never depend on someone else to make you happy. That's what alcohol is for! I do recommend waiting until you're in a good place, until the main scars have healed. Take time out to focus on you and your children before rushing in. Nobody wants the broken version of you. Fix yourself first as much as you can. When we are weak and vulnerable, we tend to make bad decisions about who is right for us, who is good for us. We accept faults in people just because they make you feel good.

Well, I'm not going to settle for that. That's probably another reason I'm still single. But that's also because I would rather live my life alone than together with another "wrong" partner. I've been single for quite a while now and I have to say it's going very well. I think *I* might be the one! I have been on more first dates than I've had hot dinners! Well not quite, but it is funny that I've had so many. I suppose over the years I see this as me continuing to search for my destined partner. He's quite elusive it seems. First dates are an opportunity to see if there is any chemistry. Something that is either there or it isn't. It's an instant feeling and only if I get that feeling would I do a second date to explore further.

There are sometimes red flags that scream at you during a first date. They will be different for everyone; one of mine is the relationship they have with their children. If they are estranged or don't see them very often, I run a mile. If they speak badly about their children then it's a no from me. I did have a mini relationship with someone who had two boys that were 15 and 18. Everything was going well until I met them at his house. The way he spoke to them and reprehended them was shocking. I witnessed this a few times and decided I would never want him to talk to my children in that way. So, I ended it.

I would always advise not talking about ex partners on a first date. Sometimes I've sat and listened to men go on and on about what a witch their ex was. They can talk about their disgust paying child maintenance payments. Now that really makes my blood boil. I remember another first date where he said that his child maintenance payments had bought his ex a new sofa. I was incensed. No, it didn't. Your ex bought a new sofa. Your payments go towards the needs of *your* children, full stop. And in my experience, that didn't even scratch the surface. I spent most of mine on childcare, especially in the early years.

So dating is an absolute minefield, and I would suggest you use the first date to assess what kind of man it is you're potentially going to see again. If you see a red flag, run a mile, ladies. Run a mile. You and your children deserve more. Learn to love the sound of your feet walking away from things not meant for you. So many good women sleep alone because they know the value of the space beside them. And remember that you can't be everyone's cup of tea, otherwise you'd be a mug!

Looking for a New Daddy...a Good One

I do think that subconsciously, I had been doing this for years, while the boys were young. I didn't want to be single for a long time and if I could just find a good man with a kind soul, he could make my family "normal" again. I have so much respect for men who can heal a heart he didn't break, and love a child he didn't make. If you did manage to find a man like that after your divorce, then I hope you realise how special that is and how lucky you are.

My viewpoint was that if I was going to spend time with someone, this precious time is time away from my children, and that needed to be worth it. Sadly, few people lived up to this high expectation I had set for myself. Going on a first date only to find out it was a waste of time is disappointing. Over time I saw it as another lucky escape from the many men who would not give me what I deserved and needed. Being pretty won't keep a man; sex won't keep a man; and a baby won't keep a man.

Heck, being a good woman barely keeps a man. The only thing that'll keep a man is a man that wants to be kept. Try to consider this in the early days of a relationship. I have found so many time wasters – men who clearly were not looking for a deep and solid long-term relationship. With practice and experience, I learnt to be aware of this and quickly move on. Be clear from the very beginning on what you're looking for. Men who just want to get a quick leg over will realise it's not worth the effort and move onto someone willing to sleep around. Once I decided I wasn't looking for a new daddy for my boys it became a little easier. But I still couldn't navigate dating successfully. There were a few times when I felt that things were going so well, then I would introduce said man to my children. Sometimes in the following weeks, I regretted doing this too early. In time I learnt to not introduce them until a significant period had elapsed. Even then, relationships can go sour.

I find it very upsetting when children are introduced to many different and frequent men. Again, there are no rules about this; you must decide yourself when this is right. I do feel that people can pretend to be someone else for three, maybe four months. Then eventually if there are any cracks, the true person is revealed. I had one guy hide from me for weeks that he was an alcoholic. In hindsight the signs were there, but only after a considerable few weeks was it apparent that he didn't have a handle on alcohol. I ended the relationship sadly when I found this out, and before any deeper feelings could develop.

I also had another mini relationship with a wonderful guy. I introduced him to my boys and after a while, we all went on a short break together. I sorted the accommodation and he said just before we set off that he didn't have any money for the trip. I paid for *everything*. He also kept making suggestions in front of the boys to do different activities, which of course I had to pay for. He encouraged the boys to have a starter, main and pudding when we ate out, which I paid for. So, it became clear that he never had any money and clearly loved spending mine. He became like a third child as I would have to pay for everything. That just wasn't sustainable and again I ended that too.

I know many women look for men with plenty of money as a priority. This I find disdainful. Yes, money is important, and I believe if you're well-matched on the money front, that works best. I've always paid my way on dates and would never expect anyone to pay for the whole evening's drinks or a full meal. I've spoken to many men on my dates who have told me awful stories about women wanting them to take them shopping, sometimes even *on a first date*! These money-grabbing women are a disgrace and an insult to womankind. It's a strength to walk away. You don't need a man to solve your problems; you just need a man who doesn't become a problem. Learn to walk away but always do it kindly and with compassion.

Divorce is OK. Breaking up is OK. Moving on is OK. Being alone is OK. What is not OK is staying somewhere you are not valued and appreciated. Never let someone show you twice that you don't matter.

Internet Dating and Being Safe

I wouldn't say I'm an expert on dating or internet dating. However, I have had quite a lot of experience on the subject. I have friends who have done a fair bit of internet dating too, and others who were on a site for only a month and met their husbands. So, although there are no guarantees, it can work. It's just one of the ways people meet these days. Even the younger generations are hooking up on dating websites or apps.

It's a culture that is widespread and has come a long way from the stigma it generated in the early days of match-making companies.

The first step is to choose one of the many sites that are available and not be scared. Choose a few recent photos and if necessary, get a friend to help you write a short bio about yourself. It's so important to be honest and certainly *not* to lie about anything, especially your age. You will find that many people lie. I have no understanding of this. Why would you start a relationship with a lie? I suppose it makes people think they will have more success. I find many men who are in their 50s say that they are 49! One guy I met I discovered was 58, not 49! Exasperating. I would also suggest that you don't include any photos with your children. You would think this was just common sense; however, you will find that common sense goes out of the window when internet dating. I've met people who look 10 years older than their photos. Again, why would you do this? I have no idea.

There are a few rules that you need to follow, especially as a woman. Safety is a big issue, and you can keep yourself safe if you follow these rules. Once you've struck up a conversation via the site with messages back and forth, and it's going well, I would suggest you have a telephone conversation before the meeting.

Talking to someone on the phone is a good way to get to know if you're on the same page. Also, it tends to help rid you of the men who are never going to talk to you on the phone and are not seriously looking for a relationship. Yes, I believe there are many men, probably married or in relationships who use dating sites for a little excitement and to chat freely with women other than their wives. You need to hunt these out and not play their game. If someone is happy to have a chat on the phone, then that's a good start. I would also recommend that you do this quickly. What is the point of sending endless messages back and forth when he has no intention of taking this further?

I know some women who chatted with men for weeks, even months and never asked to meet up. Well, you seriously don't know who you're talking to. You're building a relationship via messages with someone who could be anybody! He could be in another country. He could sadly be an internet scammer. Yes ladies, they're out there and it's real: Men from all over the world who play on the insecurities of women, building online connections for weeks and months. They shower you with compliments and sound like the perfect man.

The lady believes there is something amazing between them, but eventually, they ask for money or have some sob story, where you feel compelled to help them out. Unbelievably, women are scammed out of hundreds and thousands of pounds and this happens every single day. This is a great reason to have a phone conversation quickly. These scammers will run a mile as they have no intention of ever talking to you.

In a survey commissioned by UK Finance in 2019, it was found that over 27% of users of online dating apps were "catfished" (a fraudulent act where someone using an online dating app or service adopts a fake persona).[3] Another survey in 2021 found that nearly 40% of people looking for love online were asked for money.[4] Wow! So what can you do to protect yourself? Here are a few suggestions to keep you safe.

Ask for a Video Chat or to Meet Up.
Scammers create fake profiles, they never use their own pictures. Instead, they catfish their victims by using stolen photos of attractive individuals. They are also quick to call it love! They want to move the relationship forward as quickly as possible to make you feel like it's something real.

Once they have your trust they start to ask for things. They create elaborate stories to ask for financial help to get them out of some sort of trouble. They may ask you to send cash or gift cards or share sensitive photos. And they will *never* meet in person or video chat. This is where you have an advantage. If you suspect you're being scammed, just ask for a video chat or to meet up. Quite often they have already told you they are in a different country, so a meet-up is out of the question. If you insist on a video chat they will run a mile if they are not genuine! This is how you protect yourself, ladies!

I know it seems like a minefield, but if you are aware of scammers and cheats, you can be safe and eradicate them.

Now, it's important to understand that people will chat with you via messages and then just stop. You will never hear from them again. They have moved on to someone else. Yes, this hurts at first but try to see it as them not being right for you. When you ask to chat on the phone, some people will block you. And that's fine. They were never serious about you and could be a scammer. Lucky escape.

If They Agree to a Meetup, Never Ask Them to Pick You Up From Home.

Once you've had a conversation over the phone, if that's gone well then you can have your first date. This is where safety is super important. The golden rule is to *never* ask them to pick you up from your home. I also suggest you don't let them know where you live for at least three or four dates, at least until you've had a chance to validate their intentions. I know many women who think that they know the person well after chatting for a few weeks. They feel comfortable with the person, so they tell them where they live and get in a car with a complete stranger. Unbelievable. He could have a sledgehammer in the back. Please, please do not do this.

Always Meet Somewhere With Plenty of People Around.

A bar or a coffee shop are good, first-date venues. Don't forget to tell someone exactly where you are going. At the end of the night, go home alone. Yes, they can walk you to your car or help you to get a taxi if needed but *don't* get in their car – not even when it's gone well.

You still need to build trust. And remember, people can pretend to be anyone they want to be, especially for the first few dates. You must only open your world up when time has elapsed and you feel comfortable to do so. I even know friends who have brought a first date back to their house when their children have been asleep upstairs. You really don't know who you're inviting into your safe place or what they are capable of. So, take good care. Follow these rules and take it slowly.

Keep the Faith

There have been many times when I have become completely exasperated by internet dating. When this happens, I suggest you take a break. There are many ups and downs, and you can seem to spend hours swiping left or right. In fact, I do believe I've swiped right on most of the single men in Manchester twice over. I truly believe when the time is right, it will happen.

However, I don't know when that time will be. I often remind myself of the famous song by Michael Bublé: "I just haven't met you yet." That's how I see it. I just haven't met him yet, but I know he's out there. One day, a first date will be my last first date. I've kissed a few frogs, but my prince is coming. When I moved into the home where I raised my children as a single mum, I met a wonderful elderly lady who lived across the road from me. In true neighbourly kindness, she invited me for coffee a day or so after we moved in. I remember sitting in her spotless home and telling her about my boys, whom she really took a shine to over the following years. She adored watching them grow and was always complimentary about them. They always took the time to talk to her and make a fuss about her dog. "Look at them grow," she would say. "How tall they are now," "You've got two very handsome boys."

She, like me, had found herself alone with her two daughters when she was a similar age to me. So, although she was much older than me now, she was in the Divorce Club. She was in her late 70s, and both her daughters had their own lives. One lived far away, and she saw the other one occasionally. I asked her if she had ever remarried and was quite surprised by her response. She said she was far too busy raising her children and didn't really bother to find anyone else. By the time they had grown up, she felt it was too late for her and was quite content being on her own. I felt saddened by this. She had given everything to her daughters but was now all alone. I vowed that day to never give up the search. And although I have at times taken a significant break from the frustrations of internet dating, I always keep going and keep the faith.

Children Always Come First

> *"Of course, her kids come before you; hell, her kids come before her."*
> – Kevin Gates

This is something I feel very strongly about. When dating someone new or in any relationship after a split, *your children should always come first*. And if someone doesn't understand or appreciate that, then walk away. Look out for a man who feels the same way about their children. If they don't put their children first, this is an instant no for me. Obviously, it can be a challenge to balance a new relationship, especially when both parties have children. But you must learn to ensure that your children don't feel abandoned while you bask in the wonderful feelings of a new relationship. Remember: It may take the children longer to embrace a new man in your life. They may not instantly like him as you do. There are many challenges in a new relationship with children.

If someone expects you to put them before your children, this is a major red flag. They should be understanding of your circumstances, and help you balance their needs with the needs of the relationship. You do need to create time and space for a relationship to grow, but not at the expense of your children. Sadly, when considering any new relationships that your ex might have, you can't expect the same in return. You need to realise that you have absolutely no control over their choice of their new partner and the impact this might have on your children.

You can't control how many partners will be introduced or the timing of this. I do know some couples who have an agreement about this and communicate well together, prior to any introduction. However, I think these people are in the minority. All you can do is to help your child deal with any changes. If you have any concerns, you have every right to try to address them with your ex. Just don't expect that you will get the response you want to hear. New relationships on both sides can be difficult and quite distressing for the children involved. The only thing that will aid any difficulties is good clear and supportive communication. Which is seldom to come across, but it is possible. So, I'm told!

When You Find Love Again

The words below are so beautiful, and they sum up exactly what you need in your life. Read them and know that you are not willing to make sacrifices anymore:

> *When you fall in love, fall in love with their eyes, their smile, and the sound of their voice. Fall in love with someone who wants to know everything about you, your past, and your future. Fall in love with someone who can not only touch your body but your soul. Fall for someone whose face lights up when they see you, and they smile an honest smile, showing they are truly happy to be with you. Fall for someone who wants to know exactly how you like your coffee and how to make your favourite foods. Fall for someone whose very mention of their name brings a smile to your face and a sense of calmness over your body. Love the one who brings you happiness and a smile you can not hide. Someone who makes you feel safe and secure. Love the person who makes you feel like you do not have*

to hide anymore and no longer have to live in fear. Fall for the one you want to run to with every exciting or upsetting situation you encounter and is always *there to listen and give you faith to keep going or get just as excited as you do. The one you miss the second they walk away. Fall for the one who makes the world disappear when you're with them. Fall for the one no matter how hard you try you just cannot say goodbye or get them out of your mind. Fall for the one who is not only your significant other but your best friend, confident, and other half. Fall for the one you do not just want to sleep with but wake up to.* – Unknown

You deserve all the above. You deserve to be loved unconditionally, and to be able to express your love back unconditionally too. If you think twice about a second date, then it's a no.

Don't try to fit a square peg into a round hole. Some people will only like you if you fit inside their box. There should be no consideration, just an overwhelming feeling that you have met someone special.

And maybe, a happy ending doesn't include a guy. Maybe it's you, on your own, picking up the pieces and starting over, freeing yourself up for something better in the future. Maybe the happy ending is just moving on.

Chapter 12
I'll Take Care of Me for You, If You Take Care of You for Me

How does a child learn to walk? They watch you walking and think, I want to do that. How does a child learn to talk? They listen to you talk, encouraging them to put sounds together to form words. How does a child learn to eat? They watch you eating and do the same and you gradually ease them onto foods that are suitable for their tiny mouths.

What I'm trying to say here is that children learn to look after themselves by watching you look after yourself. Or indeed the other side of the coin is that a child can also develop the same harmful habits and traits that you display to them. It's both wonderful and tragic at the same time.

Parenting is such a massive responsibility, and we may not even notice that our words, behaviours, and actions define their words, behaviours and actions – especially when dealing with massive life-changing trauma such as divorce.

We can become so consumed by our situation that we are blind to what's going on with our little ones. All we can do is to be mindful of this and if we step off track, quickly bring ourselves back to being the role model we desire to be.

Take some time to think about all the things you do that you would like your children to copy. What are the behaviours you want them to develop that you display on a regular basis? Make a list, lists are powerful. Pop this down in your journal. Take a couple of days to think and consider and add to your list as you go along. Now, consider all the attributes and behaviours that you have displayed in front of your children that you don't want them to copy. Come on now, be honest with yourself. We've all done things in front of the children we're not proud of. We've all said things and maybe not been kind to others in their presence.

Write these things down, this is just for your eyes only, so be honest with yourself. Purely doing this exercise will help you to make a few changes, to be more mindful of your actions, and to help shield from your children the side of you that you're not proud of. I want to help you change this part of yourself. To become a better person, a person you will like a lot more. A person your children can aspire to become.

By looking after yourself for you and your children, you encourage them to look after themselves for you and for them. That's a win-win situation right there.

Self-Development Is the Best Thing You Can Give Your Kids

Working on you and your own self-development is the best gift you can give to your children. Being the best version of yourself is the best gift you can give to your children. The power of improving your life, your outlook and your thought processes has a massive impact on what you teach your children and the person they become. If they see *you* striving to be the best person you can be, they will strive to be the best person they can be. Just think about that for a while. Just like children copy how to walk and how to talk, they also copy your intent on living and your drive to improve. Your ability to push through, your love of learning about how to become a better person.

The difficult thing for us is that often they don't even notice this is happening, and neither do you. I've been inspired by many books and teachings over the years. However, when I try to show these teachings to my children they are 100% not interested. Many years ago, I came across the *Chicken Soup* books. I absolutely loved them, especially the book named *Chicken Soup for the Woman's Soul*. I was so inspired by these stories they filled my heart and soul with optimism and hope.

How amazing it was to then find out that they had also made a book called *Chicken Soup for the Teenager*. I was thrilled, so I bought this book for my eldest son. To this day, I am unsure how much of this book he has read, however just owning a book like this is power. He may pick it up from time to time, maybe he's only read a small portion of the book on the day he received it as a gift. And if he did, I know it would be a good part of the book because it's amazing throughout. But the point is he has the book, and it is there in his time of need to pick up and use for inspiration.

I consider myself to be a self-development junkie. I read no other books. Fiction and stories for me are saved for Netflix. Books are for inspiration and self-development and I love them. I've read many that I find shallow and uninspiring. Sometimes in these books, it's just one simple sentence that has "spoken" to me. And that's more than OK. That's the purpose. Not every word is significant but if one thought, one suggestion, or one point of view changes my way of thinking, then it's a winner. Now I prefer to download audio books. It's simple and makes dead time spent doing other tasks inspirational. Previously I would watch the TV while getting ready in the morning, doing my hair and makeup. Now I listen to self-development audiobooks. In the car, especially on a long journey, they are amazing. Try it. You will be amazed how this dead time becomes an amazing journey of learning and inspiration.

Often, we never know how our actions are impacting those around us. Knowing this we just need to continue with good habits, safe in the knowledge that they are rubbing off on our little ones. If not now but at some point, in their future. Maybe one day when they are 20, 30 or even 40 years old they will remember what you as their mum (or dad) used to do to grow and develop. Remember, not everything reveals itself in the moment. Some things take time, and even years. But the rewards are never-ending.

Push Your Boundaries and Comfort Zones

Your ability to grow is directly related to the amount of insecurity you can accept in your life. If you stagnate, how can you grow? Growth and change demand that you push your comfort zone sometimes to the limit. Do things you would never dare to do, take risks. I know this is scary, which is why I always say do the easy stuff first. Build on the easy actions and the bigger stuff suddenly doesn't seem too big to handle.

Courage is being afraid and acting anyway. Think back to when you were a child: Children have little fear and a zest for experience. Children learn by doing things they've never done before. When did you stop doing things you've never done before? As a child, you were doing these things almost every day. How wonderful life would be if we took that "just do it" attitude into adulthood?

Beliefs and Values For You and Your Children

I find it unbelievable that we send our children to school for many years to prepare them for this thing called "life." However, we fail to teach them some of the fundamental lessons they need to succeed. For example, how a bank account works, what a direct debit is, money management and how to avoid being in debt. How is a salary made up, what is tax and National Insurance, and why do we need to pay this? I could write a book on the many areas in which we fail our children to fully prepare for life. Most parents fill these gaps, but some children don't have anyone who can help them with these life challenges, and they have no option but to struggle through.

As you go through the early years as an adult you slowly learn what is needed. Imagine how much easier it would be if we were fully prepared and understood how to be an adult. How fewer people would get into debt if they learnt how important it was to save some of the money they earn, and how to make their money work for them instead of throwing it away.

There are two subjects that, if taught in school or early in life, would not only have an impact on children individually but on society as well. And this is an understanding of the impact of our beliefs and values on our entire life. Simply teaching this could prevent people from spiralling out of control. Understanding our negative thought patterns and how to turn this around into a positive belief system empowers your being and enables you to lead a successful and full life. You're able to gain an understanding of the strategies used to quash your limiting beliefs and replace them with a belief system that nourishes you and helps you to achieve. On top of this, imagine if we could teach our young adults to examine their personal values. By identifying our core values and living and breathing them each day, we can lead lives filled with happiness and a zest for living.

When I first came across the importance of examining our beliefs and values, it completely changed how I saw everything. I finally understood why past experiences didn't sit well with me. I understood why the moments of joy I had experienced *were* moments of joy: It was because those moments aligned with my values.

Once I understood this, I had a strategy to create more of these moments. I knew exactly the types of scenarios and situations that made my heart skip a beat. I identified and dealt with beliefs I had been carrying around for years that stopped me from moving forward positively. I analysed my limiting beliefs so that they no longer limited me. I changed my belief system to one that helped me make positive changes.

Had I known all of this at 18 when I left school, who knows how different my life could have been? But I am grateful that I learnt it, and it was the start of a lifelong journey of self-development that I could share and build on. There is so much out there to read that can bring hope in times of need, faith in times of despair and love in times of loneliness.

Defining Your Beliefs and Values

What you believe about yourself impacts what is possible both in your work and personally. What you believe about yourself can either impact your life positively or negatively.

Dealing with my belief system changed my life. I developed a new set of beliefs, which moved me forward instead of holding me back. Negative beliefs are destructive because the more we focus on them, the more we see them, and the less we see what's good about ourselves.

Often people attempt to live their lives backwards: They try to have more things or more money, to do more of what they want so that they will be happier. The way it works is the reverse. You must first be who you really are, then do what you need to do, to have what you want.

Part of finding out who you really are is working on the beliefs that you hold about yourself, which basically are not valid, although you accept them as truth. They are not really you and don't move you forward as a person.

Beliefs don't sit inside you as opinions; they come across as solid facts as they are deeply embedded inside as truths. Sometimes, negative beliefs can be a little difficult to uncover, however often, negative beliefs come flying at you from all directions.

Your Limiting Beliefs	How To Challenge Them
Everyone else can have a perfect life.	Do you believe you're not worthy?
I have always felt that I was not good enough to get the big things in life.	Do you believe you're not good enough?

I have no time do all the things I want to do.	Do you believe that you have no time for yourself?
I've never been a very confident person.	Do you believe you have no confidence?
I'm too old, too young, too lazy, too weak, not attractive, not strong, a failure, I will always be lonely, I am poor, I am quiet. I have nothing to give. I can't survive on my own. I'm not a good parent, son, daughter, friend.	Do you believe that you can't truly be happy, lose weight, stop smoking, that you have no self-discipline, that it doesn't get better than this?

The list of limiting beliefs is endless.

You may not think you hold many negative beliefs about yourself, but believe me, *you do*. Everyone does to a certain degree and most people have a variety of them. With investment in yourself and over a period of time, as you become more aware of the harmful effects of your thinking, you can begin to uncover your negative beliefs. When you believe something, you give your brain an unquestioned command to respond in a certain way. As soon as we have a belief, it begins to control what we see, what we feel, and ultimately, what we do.

I can't stress enough how important it is to spend time on your belief system. Your beliefs are a very powerful force and have a dramatic effect on your life. If you're not convinced, consider this: Beliefs can even affect your heartbeat. People who faithfully believe in voodoo believe they will die if someone puts a "hex" on them. Not because of the "hex" but because they give their own heart an unquestioned command to stop breathing. Beliefs are very powerful, so you've got to be careful about what you choose to believe, especially about yourself.

So, what is a belief anyway? Often, we talk about things without having a clear idea of what they really are. Most people treat a belief as if it's a real thing when it's nothing but a feeling of certainty about what something means. If you say you believe you're intelligent, all you're really saying is, I feel certain that I'm intelligent. That sense of certainty allows you to tap into resources that help you act intelligently to produce the results you want. We all have the answers, or at least we have access to the answers we need through others, but often our belief, our lack of certainty, causes us to be unable to use the capacity that resides within us. How many times have you *not* done something because you didn't believe you could truly do it? How many lost opportunities have you let slip through your fingers? Do you have any regrets because you didn't act? Did your belief system let you down?

Isn't it true that you have enough experience or know enough people who have gone through difficult times, that if you really wanted to, you could easily develop the belief that people are rotten? That given half a chance, they would take advantage of you? You probably don't want to believe this, it certainly won't get you anywhere, but we all have experiences that could support this idea. Isn't it also true that you have experiences that support the idea that people are basically good, and that if you truly care about them and treat them well, they will want to help you? The most important question is, which one of these is true? It's whichever belief you decide to assemble and take on board. It's your choice.

You will have thousands of beliefs, but a few major ones will be shaping the world you have created for yourself. Which beliefs do you use to guide you? On which beliefs do you base your decisions? Which of your beliefs are propelling you forward, and which are holding you back?

Our beliefs shape the direction of our lives. They come from anybody who exerts influence over us. This usually starts in childhood with your parents, then anyone who may have an influence over you – your boss, your partners, your family, your friends. Here is a technique to help you overcome the beliefs that are holding you back:

I would like you to complete six sentences that begin with the words "I MUST." Do not think too deeply about this, write down the first things that come to mind. Now ask yourself: What would happen if I didn't do these? What this does is to help you examine the consequences of various actions.

Now complete six sentences beginning with the words "I CAN'T." Then ask yourself the question, "What's stopping me?" *Keep on writing.* Write down all the limiting beliefs you keep telling yourself. Listen to the little voices in your head:

What are you not good at? What can't you do? Think about your perfect life. Why do you tell yourself you can't have it? I call this your "excuses list." These are the things that stand between you and your dream.

I have always wanted to be_____ but I can't because_____. I can't get a job because I'm too old. I can't lose weight because I don't have any self-control. I have always wanted to _____ but I can't because_____ GO ON FILL IN THE BLANKS. You do this and it could completely change your life.

Examples of disempowering beliefs:

Life is a struggle.
Nothing is ever easy.
It's out there – go get it, but it's hard work.
If you want something you've got to fight for it.
People are only out for themselves.
Once you hit forty it's downhill all the way.
Nothing is free.
Success only comes at a high price.
I must battle every step of the way.
It is not possible to have an ideal life.
You must accept the hand of fate.
Most things in life are out of your control.
I was lucky that time, but I bet I couldn't do it again.
I need more experience to get the job I want.
There is nothing I can do to get out of this situation I am in.

I would like you to highlight the negative beliefs you have identified with from what you have written here. Pick three big ones that you feel hold you back the most.

Changing your beliefs or adding new ones is possible and can happen in a remarkably short space of time. The growth of hundreds of cults around the world is a clear, if alarming, example of how effectively people can be persuaded to adopt new beliefs. Some of the more damaging cults brainwash young people into rejecting their entire lives and families. Be clear about what you want to believe and take responsibility for choosing your beliefs yourself. All it takes to confirm these new beliefs in your thinking is having an understanding of the process involved and the willpower to implement them.

Step 1: You need to want the change them!
Beliefs are deeply personal, and they shape the way you view your life. So, they can be very hard to let go. If someone is not willing to let go of a belief it becomes almost impossible to achieve different and greater results. To want to change a belief you've got to see the advantages of changing it. You've got to be able to recognise that it isn't helping you. In fact, it may even be causing you enormous problems and you've got to be able to see that there is an alternative that could work for you in a far happier and more effective way. You need to want to change your negative beliefs.

Step 2: Open yourself to the possibility.
The next step is to accept the idea that it can be changed. To allow that it is possible. Most people see their current beliefs

as facts, simply the way things are and unchangeable. This doesn't mean that you must believe that changing your beliefs is possible. All you must do is be willing to put your disbelief to one side. This will give you the space in which to be flexible and allow change to unfold. Oprah Winfrey says, "I don't think of myself as a poor deprived ghetto girl who made good. I think of myself as somebody who, from an early age, knew I was responsible for myself and that I had to make good." Think of the dramatic impact of these two beliefs and the sort of life each person would have who held these differing beliefs.

Here is a great example of what a belief can do. In May 1954 Roger Bannister ran a mile in three minutes and 59.4 seconds. The news of this immediately flashed around the world. For hundreds of years, runners had tried unsuccessfully to run a mile in under four minutes. Scientists and doctors said it couldn't be done. So, what made it possible for Bannister to do the impossible? Why did he succeed where others had failed? The answer is quite simple. He chose to set aside the global belief that it wasn't possible and to believe in his goal. More interestingly, within seven months thirty-seven more runners had done it too. In the next three years three hundred more. Because the whole world now believed it was possible. Step two is to open yourself to the possibility that it can be changed.

Step 3: Take responsibility.
There's absolutely no point blaming circumstances or other people for your life now. Blame will simply keep you stuck

and feeling like a victim. Taking responsibility is liberating. However, it doesn't mean blaming yourself either, it means recognising that you can choose to change it and create the life you really want. You don't need anyone or anything else to change; you don't have to depend on others or to wait for a lucky break. You can go out and make your own lucky break right now.

"You can have what you want, or you can have your excuses for not having it."
– Jen Sincero

Excuses are easy to make. I have made many and still do. But they're not a lot of fun when they're a substitute for action and success. To help you with this, look at your empowering beliefs. How have they helped you achieve and succeed in your life so far? See these beliefs as natural assets that will help you with whatever you have to face.

Step 4: Eliminate your disempowering beliefs.
It's time to question the validity of these, to pick them up, give them a good shake and begin to undermine the hold they have over you. Look at your three most disempowering beliefs.

Ask yourself the following questions:

Where did that belief come from?
Who gave you that belief?
How do you feel about the person that gave you that belief?

Do you respect them? Are they always right?
How is this belief ridiculous?
What does this belief cost me daily?
What will the long-term cost be if I don't let go of this belief?
How will your life be different daily if you let this belief go?

These questions begin to weaken your negative beliefs. Now take each belief and replace it with the opposite i.e., "I'm too old to change my career" becomes "This is the perfect age to consider a change and I bring to my new career my wealth of life experience." Take some time out from reading this book to do this exercise.

Coming up with your new beliefs should be fun, make them as strong as possible. To weaken your negative beliefs further, look for evidence to disprove them. Then look for evidence to prove your new beliefs. Look for stories and examples of people starting a new career aged 35 and over, and look online at the many people who have done what you want to do. They *are* out there. The evidence is there, you simply weren't looking for it before. You were looking for evidence to support your old belief system instead.

Write DELETE across your old beliefs. That's the way I used to be and this is the way I am now. Write your new set of empowering beliefs down. Make your new beliefs visible, somewhere you can see them every day. Maybe stick them on the fridge or your bathroom mirror. Even if you don't 100% believe it yet. *Don't give up, keep seriously questioning your beliefs.* Are they realistic?

My old belief system was extremely destructive. I believed I was unattractive, not confident, and that my life had no hope. I couldn't make it on my own, I was a weak person with no staying power, and life was a struggle. I had no self-worth. No wonder my life was a mess. Over time I replaced them and now, I don't believe any of these things anymore.

Low confidence is a very common limiting belief. This often arises due to someone else telling us we are not good at something. The more they tell us, the more we believe it. This is what I call confidence abuse, even though in reality our confidence hasn't been taken away. We have let it go. We have given away our power to someone else. Our lack of confidence can also come when we constantly compare ourselves to others. Instead of aspiring to be like that person, we beat ourselves up about how we could never do what they do.

For example, my ex-husband would tell me I couldn't cook. He said it frequently and I started to believe it. My mind started looking for proof of this, and once it's gathered enough evidence, *bang!* It's in the bag. Where it gets dangerous is when people tell us we are stupid, unattractive, we can't socialise or communicate, we're too old, we will never lose weight, we're too small. Once we realise this, we have a responsibility to be careful how we contribute to the negative beliefs of others. Words can be the sharpest blade or a fatal bullet in the minds of others.

Once we've broken down our negative beliefs, what helps to make the change to believing our new belief is working with affirmations. An affirmation is an empowering sentence that we say to ourselves as many times as possible throughout the day. We feed our conscious and subconscious minds with what we choose to believe about ourselves and what our subconscious mind does is go out there and look for evidence that we *are* right.

I am beginning to discover just how wonderful I am.
I decide to be me, I approve of myself as I am.
I choose to love and enjoy myself.
I live in the now, each moment is new. I choose to see my self-worth and I love and approve of myself.
There is always a new and better way for me to experience life.
Intelligence, courage, and self-worth are always present.
I know I am worthwhile; it is safe for me to succeed.
I easily and comfortably release that which I no longer need in my life.
I am filled with joy; it flows through me with every beat of my heart.
There is time and space for everything that I need to do, I am at peace.
I am free of all irritations, all is well.
I create only peace and harmony within myself and my environment. I deserve to feel good.
I forgive others, I forgive myself, I am free to love and enjoy life.
I now choose to support myself in loving joyous ways.
I move beyond old limitations and now allow myself to express myself freely and creatively.

Make your own up! What's important with affirmations is that you don't give up after two days or two weeks. It takes time and effort to make improvements in your life, but you are worth it. And it will set you free.

Your Two Conflicting Minds

So, we have established that the world you live in is determined largely by what goes on in your mind. Marcus Aurelius, the great Roman philosopher said, "A man's life is what his thoughts make of it." Additionally, Ralph Waldo Emerson, America's foremost philosopher said, "A man is what he thinks all day long." Both of these men realised that the beliefs, thoughts and expectations that we habitually entertain will actualise themselves in the physical conditions of our world. *The mind attracts to it whatever it has been conditioned to attract.* The biggest person you will ever have to overcome in your life is *you* and what you believe about yourself.

Your Positive Self and Your Negative Self
We all have two sides: a positive side and a negative side. Mostly we go through life without any knowledge of this. However, for a happy balanced life, it is important to manage both of these "sides." It's especially essential to keep your negative side under control. It's easy to be negative. It takes little strength to leave them roaming around in your mind. Your negative side will overthrow any hope of positive you have inside you. Once you learn to control your mind, it's a game changer.

Positive Self: Guides you towards life's blessings	Negative Self: Expects failure
Love	Poverty
Friendship	Ill Health
Success	Doubt
Creativity	Fear
Happiness	Criticism
Abundance	Loss Of Love
Confidence	Old Age

The Riches of Life

True wealth lies in a positive mental attitude, labour of love, harmony of home and relationships, sound physical health, freedom of fear, self-discipline, play, self-discovery of one's self, faith, and inner peace.

The only thing you have total control over in your life is what you are feeling right now. You have total control over your heart and your mind. How you choose to control them now and every minute of the day, and tomorrow and every day of your life has a direct impact on your future. Changing your beliefs for a better life takes 100% commitment. Some days you will be despondent and think that you are fooling yourself. Other days you will be high on the new possibilities that open themselves to you.

It's a journey of ups and downs, but it does have a dramatic difference in your life. It may take a while, especially if your belief is deeply embedded, but once you start to disprove one, the others become easier to work with as you now believe that it *is* possible. Work with your new belief, repeat your affirmations and most importantly take positive action on the areas of your life you want to improve.

It's a little like doing a jigsaw without seeing the picture. All the pieces fit together with time, commitment, and a positive belief system. If you try this and still feel that something is holding you back or blocking you, it may be worth thinking about seeing a counsellor. Maybe there is a specific problem from your past, which needs to be dealt with before you move on with your future. I dealt with a specific problem unsuccessfully for 20 years. It wasn't until I had a one-hour session with a counsellor that from that very moment, it was gone – transformed in my mind into a completely new way of thinking. And that new thinking or belief has stayed with me to this day. It ran so deep that I needed someone to help me to deal with it. And they did.

What Are Your Core Values?

By taking the time to clarify the values that form your "core", you can add more meaning and passion to your everyday life. One of the common themes I see in people is a desire to explore what they are truly meant to do with their lives. Most of us have a sense that there is a better, more meaningful way to live our lives, but we can't seem to find it by ourselves. We carry on doing what is required of us, but still, this nagging sense that "there must be something more" returns. This search for a greater sense of their life's purpose underlies questions such as:

> How can my career or work be more fulfilling?
> How can I find more meaning in my life?
> How can I discover what will get me fired up again?

To find the best path forward, you must first look back. To find your purpose in the most meaningful course for your life, start by looking back at those special activities or experiences that gave you a heightened sense of being alive. When you felt like you were making a difference, you were a winner or had the experience that time either disappeared or flew quickly by. These experiences always point to your underlying values.

A Fulfilled Life = A Life Aligned to Your Values

Here is a simple yet powerful truth: A more fulfilling life is simply a life where you more fully honour your values. In other words, a life that is more in line with what is most important to you. To your heart and your soul. Let your core values be the compass that guides you. When you know your core values and use them to guide your decision making, you can expect your fulfilment to increase dramatically. It is just that simple.

Discovering your core values and living a purposeful, meaningful life, is one of the greatest adventures you can embark on. Living true to yourself is the only answer. It is important to at least identify your basic core values and create a platform for your life. I want you to not only live in accordance with your values, but I also want you to find your authenticity. Your authentic self is the one who has removed outside influences from defining themselves.

So, what are your core values? These are emotional states that you want to have more of.

Below are some examples:

Achievement	Growth	Productivity
Adventure	Health/Wellness	Recognition
Ambition	Honesty	Relationships
Aesthetics/Beaut	Honour	Resilience
Authenticity	Hope	Respect
Bliss	Humility	Responsibility
Caring	Integrity	Results
Challenge	Joy	Risk-Taking
Charity	Justice	Romance
Commitment	Kindness	Safety
Contribution	Knowledge	Security
Confidence	Laughter	Self-Worth
Compassion	Leadership	Serenity
Creativity	Learning	Service
Dignity	Location	Simplicity
Discovery	Love	Sharing
Elegance	Loyalty	Strength
Equality	Mastery	Spirituality
Empowerment	Nobility	Success
Excellence	Nurturing	Teaching
Experience	Orderliness	Tradition

Faith	Originality	Trust
Family	Passion	Truth
Forgiveness	Peace	Understanding
Freedom	Personal	Vitality/Zest
Friendship	Expression	Wealth
Fun	Possibilities	Wholeness
Generosity	Potential	Wisdom
Giving	Power	Wonder/Awe

Most of us can probably say that we value most of these. However, what we are trying to find out is which values you *need* to live by each day. Which ones are the most important for you? Which ones make you feel uncomfortable if you're not living by them? We all know someone who is a natural comedian, the life and soul of a party who has the ability to make people laugh. One core value of a person like that is probably "laughter" – this person needs to laugh daily. Now if you take this person away from an environment where they can do this, a part of them will slowly die inside.

What I want you to do is to establish what you need to feel and do each day to feel alive and true to yourself. I now know that one of my core values is "security." Being aware of this helps me understand why I feel uncomfortable when I don't feel secure. This helps me to control my feelings instead of panicking like I did previously. I need to know where I stand and feel secure in my life, and therefore being aware of this helps me to consciously make decisions that make me feel more secure.

I worked for a time in my early twenties for a local newspaper, and each month I was asked to sell advertising space that I knew would not add value to my customers. The sole purpose of this activity was to hit a monthly target. I was asked to tell our customers that the money they were spending was going to a charity supported by the newspaper. However, it wasn't being donated to charity. It was to make up the financial numbers at the end of the month. People around me didn't seem to have a problem with this, but I felt very uncomfortable.

That's because I now know that one of my core values is "honesty," and my job at that time conflicted with my core values. I learnt that to be happy I needed to feel that my work was honest. And personally, I knew I needed to be honest in every part of my life. Your values express you at your core. If you've been longing to do something for a long while, it's probably a core value waiting to be expressed. Your values are about what you are naturally attracted to doing and being. When you are expressing your values, you are your most fulfilled. Your values are what call you, whether you can make money at it or not. However, when you are expressing your values and getting paid for it, you are succeeding at no emotional cost to you. Work doesn't feel like work; work becomes you.

How Do You Uncover Your Core Values?

Think about what you love to do, personally and professionally. What gives you a kick? Writing, talking, communication, painting, sport, gym, music, or any activity. Think about who you naturally are to other people – a teacher, motivator, nurturer, leader, follower, and listener. What are the qualities you need to express within yourself or your life to feel happy?

Write down your answers, then consider them: What values are expressed here? There is no right and wrong here. This is about *you*. For example, if you enjoyed painting at school you may have been expressing beauty or creativity as your value.

Decide which values are essentially you. Pick the top three values that are most precious to you – these are your core values.

A teacher I once knew identified that her core values were communication, community (voluntary work) and security. She realised that she was expressing her values at work as she loved her job. But her values were not being expressed at home. She was financially secure, but not in her relationship. Her partner was away often at the weekends doing the things he loved, like paragliding or on his motorbike. I asked her to try to establish his core values through the same process. She felt that his values were adventure, risk and freedom. These were very conflicting to her own. His honouring of his own values made her feel rejected and insecure in her relationship. If she was going to ask for her values to be nourished at home, she would have to give something in return. She became more understanding of his reasons to do crazy things and he made more effort to show her how important she was to him through communication.

The key here is communicating your values, you can't change your core values. They are as much a part of you as your DNA. But you can learn to communicate what your needs are and be mindful of the needs of others. Share them with your partner, children, friends, family and anyone who is significant in your life. Learn what your partner's core values are and the people who are close to you. People close to you need to be aware of what you need to survive on a daily and weekly basis. How do you need to feel? Do you need to feel secure, loved, and confident? Do you need to communicate, influence, and discover?

Once you are happy with your core values, being aware of them makes the decision-making process easier. Ask yourself, does this decision have a beneficial effect on my values? If the answer is yes, just do it. This applies especially when considering a new career or a new relationship. You need to honour your core values on a weekly or if possible daily basis. Brainstorm ways that you can express your values. You need to honour them at work and at home. Aligning your values to your life doesn't have to mean changing your work. Yes, you may have to do this, but maybe not. If for some reason you can't do this or can't do this now, you need to find more ways to compensate in your personal life. Also, if you don't work, it's important that your core values are nourished as much as possible throughout your day.

So, to recap on values:

Establish your core values.

Base your decisions on your core values.

Share your core values with the important people in your life, and ask for what you need.

Understand others' core values and try to honour them.

Express your core values in every area of your life, and if possible express them daily.

I've regularly asked you throughout this book to stop reading and to "do the work." If you've taken my advice here, well done to you. Give yourself a big pat on the back. However, I suspect most of you have continued reading, maybe with good intention of going back. I've done this many times when reading books only to find that I seldom return to "do the work."

This is where I have to insist that you STOP! Defining your values and diminishing your self-limiting beliefs is the *most* important positive step you can take to live a more fulfilling worthwhile life. We were not put on this earth to eat shit and die. Change your story, don't die with regret. Invest time in yourself. Don't strive to get from A to C, strive to get from A to Z. Don't compromise a life worth living because you want to get to the end of this book quicker. If you live to be 80 years old, that's 4,000 weeks in a lifetime. If you're already at 40 years old, you have 2,000 weeks left to live. By 60, you will have 1,000 weeks to live.

Make a decision on how to live with purpose, and do the bloody work, ladies. Live, love, and laugh with intention. This requires a deeper understanding of yourself. I will step off my high horse here and trust you value yourself enough to *do the f*cking work.*

Chapter 13
The New Beginning

"What a wonderful thought it is that some of the best days of our lives haven't happened yet."
– Anne Frank

I had been struggling to find the change needed for me to fully recover from my divorce years. I've tried letting my tears out, I've tried to find my peace, I've tried to meditate and dabbled with the Laws of Attraction. Each time I just couldn't shift the deep and sickening feeling from the dark pit of my stomach. I had good days and bad days, good months and bad months. And even when most parts of my life were happy, I still couldn't seem to break free.

One year yet another short relationship had abruptly come to an end. Everyone around me seemed to be happy with partners, getting married, building homes together and raising beautiful families together. I was so low I cried inside most of the day while trying to mask my dark mood from my boys, probably unsuccessfully. Later that night when I went to bed, I cried a lot under the covers of my lonely double bed, so my boys couldn't hear. I wept for myself and my situation. I decided that desperate night that I needed to make some changes. I didn't want to waste my time on dating apps, trying to meet losers who, after three months would disappoint me. I'd had years of this, and I couldn't keep doing this to myself anymore.

I also decided that I just needed to focus on me and my boys, with few distractions of things that made me sad inside. Facebook was the next app to go, I didn't delete it, but I put it on the back page of my phone, so it wasn't constantly visible to me. Too many times each day I would scroll through, wasting valuable minutes and hours watching the amazing things that my close and distant friends were doing. Romantic holidays with husbands and partners, family outings and trips, people saying how amazing their life was, their beautiful homes, new cars and so on. Each day I inflicted this on myself, and at times it made me extremely jealous and conscious of the things I *didn't* have.

It was time for me to solely focus on me and my boys, and to work hard at my relatively new job so that I had the financial security to give my boys what they needed. It was that simple, so that's what I did.

Things got better. Yes, I wondered what my friends were doing each day and I didn't know who was doing what. But focusing just on me, my boys and work slowly took me to a better place. I had no distractions that could send my mood spiralling out of control and fill me with envy. My days were lighter somehow, I wasn't chained to my phone. In fact I didn't pick it up much at all in those first few weeks.

After about two months, things were pretty good, I was working hard and looking after my boys. They were the *only* important aspect of my life. It was a short time after that I was invited out for a friend's birthday. We had a meal and ended up in a local pub where I met someone. Our eyes met across the room, and within a few minutes, he had made his way over to the bar for a chat. Was I really meeting someone the "old fashioned way"? I love that.

It's important to note here that since my divorce I'd had quite a few first dates and just a few mini relationships that all went the same way. It was usually always good in the beginning, with me getting excited that maybe this was "the one." However, over time I built a strong belief that people can be anyone they want to be for a few weeks. Sure enough after a while, the "bad stuff" comes out and they all hugely disappoint you in the end. Each mini relationship ended within the first three months.

It became a bit of a joke. Can Ang possibly manage to get this relationship over three months? In some relationships, I felt that this person was brought into my life as a lesson – a lesson for them. I usually helped them deal with some big issue or think differently about things. I felt and believed that I was a catalyst to help people get to a better place. But my heart kept being wounded along the way. I even had one guy cry at the table in a restaurant as I was counselling him on getting over his ex-wife. At times I was happy to do this but I was weary of this never-ending cycle now.

I thought the guy I had met the "old fashioned" way was going to be different, but I always remained cautious, and deep down I was waiting to uncover something that would prove to me that he was no good for me. Sure enough, this happened about two months in. He had a problem with alcohol, and although he had tried to hide this from me, eventually it surfaced. I gave him a few chances as he begged me to stay and promised he would change but he couldn't do it. The last thing me and my boys needed was an alcoholic, so it was best to get out now before he captured my heart. If I allowed myself to get deeper into this relationship, it would be much harder to walk away.

I always did the walking away, I always uncovered what was wrong with them. Afterwards, I knew it would be a good few months of endless first dates before I would meet anyone worthy of a second date. Good men were just so hard to find, all taken, were sat at home with a wife and children they adored. They were not on dating apps that's for sure.

I knew exactly what I didn't want in a man and I knew it would take someone extremely special to help me heal my broken heart. I believed he was out there, that he was hard to find, but that one day I would meet him.

Life went on, daily struggles, working hard and enjoying my boys. They were amazing and were always the best constant awesomeness in my life. I had so much love for them and felt so much love back from them. I was thankful that these many years alone and the void of a partner gave me the best relationship with my boys. They were and are my life, and because of this, we are all super close. I wouldn't have that closeness with them if I'd had a partner all these years. I know that 100%. My life was totally about my boys and I reaped the benefits of that by the solid and deep relationship we have among us. I am so grateful for that.

Nonetheless, the one area of my life I just couldn't overcome was the divorce. The way I felt about my ex-husband. I had tried, but you can't force these things. I didn't know what more I could do. It has been many years, my boys have a good relationship with him now, it was all good. But I wasn't all good, and I didn't know how to fix it. Maybe I was meant to carry this burden around with me my whole life. Maybe it's something you never get over. How do you move on when someone has deeply wounded you?

One day, I was speaking to a good friend, a fellow divorcee. Although we didn't see each other very often, whenever we did meet for coffee or wine it was almost like therapy. We both felt this, we connected over our shared troubles and issues with divorce and truly helped each other through our turbulent times. She was still consumed by turmoil at the hands of her ex, and I was so grateful that I didn't have the ongoing issues and difficulties to deal with. However, I shared with her my feelings, struggles and frustration that I just couldn't move on.

I told her that when I saw him I felt a deep sickly pit in my stomach. I hated seeing him at my front door when he walked the boys home after visits. We hardly exchanged words as I handed him back some items of my son's clothes. He at times, would try to make a funny comment and be light-hearted, but I was like stone. It was very matter-of-fact. I just couldn't stand the sight of him. Afterwards, I would close the door and feelings of anger, pain, criticism, envy and frustration would overcome me. After a while I was OK. But every week, I went through this, sometimes twice a week.

My friend gave me some great advice for my situation. Just a simple question. She asked, "Why do you have to see him?" I thought for a while. *Mmmm*, I realised that I didn't! I could take back control of the situation. The boys could let themselves in, they had a key. My son could give his clothes back to his dad. I could stay in my house and just let my boys walk in. So, that's what I did. I spoke to both boys and just said that when your dad brings you home, do you mind just letting yourselves in? I said it would be easier for me not to see him. They both understood this, probably because they found the interaction at the door uncomfortable too.

So, I deleted dating websites, social media, and my ex from my life. It felt good. I was more in control and I wasn't going to allow things that negatively impacted how I felt.

A few weeks passed, and work was great but exhausting and hard. I was building a team of people and recruiting new managers. During one interview with a lovely lady that I went onto employ, we discovered that we both had a love of personal development books. We had read a few of the same books – on positive thinking, how to be the best you can be etc. She mentioned some books I had not read, and I made a note of the titles.

I had very little time to read, however, I used my journey to work to listen to audiobooks. It's amazing how easily you can get through a book while driving to and from work. I used an app on my phone, and I would download books from the internet. I searched for one of the titles I had jotted down on my yellow Post-It note: *The Secret* by Rhonda Byrne. To my surprise, it said that I had already purchased this book. I checked the list of books on my app and sure enough, there it was at the very bottom of the list. I must have purchased it a good few years ago, and never listened to it. I must have liked the book or found something interesting about it, but I had forgotten it was even there. At the time I didn't realise the significance this book was going to have on my life.

I started listening and the book's beginning was talking about a great "secret" – a secret that people had kept and not shared for hundreds of years. A secret that could change everything in your life, and that once I learnt what this secret knowledge was, I could change anything I wanted to.

I was a little sceptical but being a very positive person, I was inwardly quite excited about what I was going to hear. This was just what I needed. Many books in the past have helped me in different ways. What was this "secret"? I couldn't wait to find out.

> *Everyone has something they want to either change or improve their life. Maybe it's a better job. Maybe it's more security. Maybe it's love. Changing your life may feel impossible. Where would you even start? With the principles of The Secret, you will learn to use the power of your mind to make what you want a reality. Through practical steps and guidance for how to shift your feelings and behaviours to a stronger, more positive place, you will learn how to harness the Law of Attraction to create a better, happier life.*[5]

Basically, *The Secret* focuses on the Laws of Attraction and positive thought processes. Previously I had not 100% been open to this prospect, or maybe I just had too much going on to fully embrace it. But I do believe reading this book was a catalyst to truly being able to move on from my divorce. Or maybe it was just the right time, or that enough time had passed to finally start letting go and become the Angela of old. Things finally started to get better.

I had spent a few years contemplating and intending to capture my divorce years on paper. But when I found the urge to do it, within a few short weeks it was done. I had replayed those terrible times and let my emotions flow into the page. I trawled through the many official court pages I had kept stored in a large box, remembering times and feelings I had buried deep in my gut. It was cathartic and painful, yes, but for me, a necessary documentation of a significant period in my life. No longer a memory but captured in the pages of my laptop. It was sad, it was heart-rending to read, but it was also my past and my truth.

Now to write about the good stuff, the positive outlook of how to get on with life, the happy ending to my tale. Detailing what I now know about life, about moving on and about happy endings, about *The Secret* and how it had a positive effect on my life.

This is where I got stuck. Many great things have happened to me, but I couldn't find the words to inspire people. The purpose of my book was not to just detail the murky and painful waters of divorce, but to inspire people that life after divorce could be amazing.

Why could I not find the words or inclination to finish my masterpiece? What more life did I have to live before I could do this?

Life was good, it had been for a while, I had discovered the teachings of *The Secret* and was learning about living by the Laws of Attraction. It made sense. I knew what I wanted, and where I had been going wrong. I was exhilarated to build my perfect life, to create it in my mind, to manifest it and to live it.

But still, no words came to inspire and incite positive energy in those who would read my words one day. Why? I did not know. I only knew that one day these words would come; I just needed to live a little more to find them.

Maybe a few months, maybe a few years. But one day I will pen more of my story.

The Good Stuff

I had been listening to the Ultimate John Rohn Library in the car one day, bored with the radio on a long journey to work. Through his words, I had an epiphany! I had resigned myself to "one day." To waiting for my next moment, for the inclination to write again. To wait to achieve my perfect life before I thought I had anything to give. Surely, I had to prove my philosophies before I could share them with the world? I had limited myself to not having anything truly valuable until I had my perfect life, partner, house, work, and fortune. Only then would little me have anything of value to give.

But this was so incorrect. Life is a journey; we are all on an amazing journey. The real essence and greatness of any journey is what you learn and what you do while you are on it. Most importantly this journey is the journey of life; it does not end, we forever grow, and we forever have value to give. Once I realised this, I asked myself, why I was not acting *now*?

Maybe because procrastination was easier than action. No action and waiting for the perfect time, day, or moment is the best excuse we have *not* to act. Not to make our dreams come true. I didn't want to get to a point in my life where I regretted not acting now, leaving it too late to get my message out there. I did have something to give. I had a philosophy on life. It might not be as awesome as John Rohn's philosophy. But I had something to share, so why not take action and share it?

I started to think about all the personal development and learning material that I had digested over the years. The people, books, philosophies, sayings, and nuggets of gold that gave me strength. Did it matter that I have not yet ended my journey? Absolutely not.

This gave me a new outlook on my book. With a new drive to act, to pen what I already have in me, despite not knowing if it was good enough. I started to piece together the essence of me. The Ultimate Ang Allan-Burns Library. It felt good. Maybe my mojo had returned, my own personal value. My story and my life are not defined by my divorce but by my values, learnings, and experiences. And when I started to piece this together, I realised I had something to say. And it was my journey so far.

I became focused on ending my book, taking action and not falling into the trap of "one day"! Because "one day" never comes. I know that now. I've always known that inside. The truth is, it's easier to put off from tomorrow to next week, to next month to next year, until one day you find yourself with one big regret. A regret is something that you look back on that you have no opportunity to change. The thought of one day regretting not completing my book, and it being too late for me to do anything about it was soul-destroying. I couldn't and wouldn't let that happen. Only I could do this; I had to find the discipline every day not to procrastinate, not to do what's easy. Not to waste my valuable time on the sofa watching mindless TV for an hour or two at night, but to be the difference I wanted to make in the lives of others as well as my own.

I had listened to the story of a man who was asked how much his television had cost him. He said it cost about £800. "Really £800?" He was then questioned about this and was asked how much his TV cost him to own it, not to buy it. Confused, the man insisted it cost £800.

Then the challenge was put to the man that the TV probably cost him around £30,000 or more each year, in fact probably well over £30,000. At first, this concept seemed ridiculous. Then it was explained that the TV time he used each day – 2, 4 even 6 hours of TV – was valuable time, that if invested in personal growth, learning a new skill, working on a business idea or doing something to help you grow could, over time could reap great rewards and financial gain.

WOW. Another epiphany right there. Imagine what you could achieve if you spent the time you invested in watching TV to something that could impact your life positively. Think of the possibilities. Think about what could be achieved. We all complain that we don't have the time to do the things we want to. We work hard and are constantly busy. But usually, at the end of the day, we let our dreams fade with mindless TV. In fact, we all have the time, we just don't have the inclination to make a massive change, to invest in ourselves, to do something different. Powerful stuff when you think of a TV in this way. Since I had a new awakening to this philosophy, I now use the TV for music, the background to me pouring my heart and soul into the book you're reading now.

I'm not saying here that you need to do the same. But maybe if you change your thinking, you can change the limiting beliefs you have about the time available to you. To act, to pursue your dreams, to make a difference. Discipline is everything and a TV is just one of the many excuses we have in our lives, consciously or unconsciously, *not to take action*.

With my renewed energy and passion for endless possibilities, I started to think about building my own personal philosophies as I look back over the years to what I have discovered.

Like when I had my first son. He was about six months old when a difficult series of events consumed my life in quick succession. I had the break-up of a difficult and traumatic relationship with his dad, rendering me a new and single mum. I found a lump in my breast shortly afterwards and with all of this going on I then heard the devastating news that as a single mum, I was being made redundant. I spiralled out of control and a complete nervous breakdown shortly followed.

My saviour was life coaching. After a very bleak and dark period of negative despair, that fighting spirit I've come to know well over the years (and especially through my divorce) shone a light within me, and I found something to give me hope.

I decided to do a course in life coaching and used this new learning to work on my own life. I learnt how to fix my life, and over time, I helped other people do the same. After learning the principles of working on your life I developed my first philosophy. I set up a life coaching business and shared my story, gave hope and helped people make positive changes in their lives. It was empowering and extremely fulfilling. And I was quite good at it.

I called my philosophy and business "Tictokology": the science of how best to spend your time. Life coaching is about devoting time to develop and work on your life each week, or even each day if you can. It's about making small simple changes that, over time, helps you to work on the more significant and difficult areas you need to work on.

I learnt about limiting beliefs, and how the things we believe about ourselves and what's possible in our life can have a major impact on what you can achieve. I learnt about personal values and how significant this was in forming a life that enriched your values rather than going against them. I learnt how to use coaching and the "grow" model to help people come to their own answers about what to do, how to act and how to create their future.

Through this, I built myself back into a good strong space. I once again felt powerful and was helping others to do the same. However, this was not what my life would continue to be. Looking back, I now know that this was the very beginning of my personal development journey. And this period of my life gave me the initial skills I would certainly need later in life. I do think that learning about life coaching at that time saved me, and continued to save me many times. It gave me the tools I desperately needed when life seemed unbearable. It gave me hope that if I had transformed my life from destruction and devastation once, I could do it again, and again, and again. And I have done this many times.

So, the foundation was set for my philosophies that could then be further developed over the years through my experiences and through my children.

The journey of Angela's philosophies on life, sprinkled with insight from many books I have read, though some of them I totally own and take all the credit for. I hope you've enjoyed reading these, so here are a few more for you!

More of Ang's Philosophies on Life

Focus on Your Core Genius

It's easy to overlook how special we are. We don't often recognise our strengths; we choose rather to consider our faults. We compare ourselves to others and destroy our self-worth. In the fake world we now live in, we imprint onto our psyche endless images from the internet and social media that make us feel totally inferior. All around us, we see celebrities and social influencers who have perfect lives.

Really? Let's have a reality check on this. The internet may have given us a whole world of information at our fingertips, but the dark side of it impacts how we feel about ourselves. And it is extremely damaging. I've seen "influencers" hiring a space for those all-important selfies that make it look like they're flying a private jet. In reality, it's a box room for hire. Really? How shallow must you be that you pretend to have a perfect life? To find your worth, you need to remove yourself from these false images and focus on your core genius. Yes, *your genius*.

What is great about you? What do you excel in? What do others say about you that is brilliant? Write down all your strengths. If you struggle with this, ask a few close friends and family members to write a list of all the amazing things about *you*! You will be surprised at what people see in you that you take for granted. Use this list to feel good every day. When you're feeling down revisit this list. With it, decide what course of action you are going to take in your life. When we use our natural skills and talents for work, that equals success and contentment.

Alongside your strengths, you need to also consider what you enjoy doing. When are you at your happiest? How do you love to spend your time? What activities do you do where time seems to stand still? When are you totally in the moment and living your best life? Do more of the things you love, and you will naturally be happier. Furthermore, if you can combine your strengths and core genius with what you love to do, you've hit the jackpot.

You can either make a salary or design a life. The greatest source of unhappiness is self-unhappiness: the unhappiness we inflict on ourselves. Let's stop, stop, *stop* making ourselves miserable. Remember the Red Cars and Blue Cars? The greatest source of our unhappiness comes from our own negative thoughts, the things we say to ourselves inwardly, all the thoughts we have in our minds. It's time to take note of the negative self-talk and stop self-destructing. Feed your mind and thoughts with positive affirmations. Talk to yourself with love and kindness. When those negative thoughts come, tell them to leave. Only you can change the way you think. In fact, the only thing we have 100% control over in our lives is what we think, what we choose to do and how we perceive the world around us. You can choose to have positive thoughts and take positive action, but it takes work and dedication. Why? Because we have endured many years of running negativity through our heads and in conversations with ourselves. Sometimes every minute of the day!

To really master this, you must think with awareness. By that I mean spend a few days learning to become more aware of the things you say to yourself each day. You will find that *you* give yourself negativity all day every day. This is what's stopping you and stifling your progress. This is the route of all your unhappiness. Once you recognise this, you can then make a choice to work with your thoughts. Train your brain to sweep away the negative and fill it with positivity. This is *hard*. I will say that again, this is *hard*. You may do it for a few days and feel like a weight has been lifted. You may be embarrassed by your self-destruction. This will be a lightbulb moment. However, beware, because the mind has been conditioned for so long, the negativity creeps back in abundance. It takes 67 days to change a habit, so commit to at least two months of practising this every day. If you do this, I know you will be happier at the end of it. Trust me, this works. But you've got to put in the effort to refocus your grey matter.

Affirmations: Words of Power

An affirmation is an idea, phrase or thought that you tell yourself. Remember when you were a child and people would tell you how good of a job you did or how much you were improving? This is an affirmation. As adults, people seldom tell us how good we are, which is why it's important to feed ourselves with positivity. You can do this inwardly, though its super powerful if you can say it out loud. I often do this in the car while driving. I would recommend you don't do this when others are around in case, they think you some crazy self-indulgent crackpot.

Here is the affirmation I use:

> *"I am whole, perfect, strong, powerful, loving, harmonious and happy, slim, beautiful, healthy, wealthy and wise."*

I know, it certainly packs a punch, doesn't it? I say this to myself quite often but especially when I'm feeling low. I also use it before doing something challenging as a sort of energy and confidence booster. It really does work.

I suggest you come up with your own personal affirmation. What do you want to believe about yourself? What positive talk do you want to feed yourself with each day? Also, you don't have to believe this, not yet anyway. Over time if you continue saying it to yourself, it becomes more and more believable.

A Few Suggestions

I am an amazing gift to myself, my friends, and the world.

I feel the love of others who are not around me.

I love and appreciate myself. I am who I am, and I love myself.

I do not need the company of others to feel complete. I am more than enough. I enjoy being in my own solitude.

The past no longer matters. It has no control over me. What only matters is the present. What I do in the present will shape my future. The past has no say in this.

Everything that I need will be provided to me at the right time and in the right place.

I believe in myself and I believe in the path I have chosen. I cannot choose the obstacles in my way, but I can choose to continue on my path because it leads to my goals.

I am not only enough; I am more than enough. I also get better every day I live. Tomorrow I will be a better version of myself than I was today.

I am happy with who I am. I am in my own skin. I am enough.

I am a smart, capable, brilliant woman, and I have everything I need to get through this.

When I make it through this, I will be better for it.

I am safe and I am well. I am healthy and I am loved.

About Time

Time is the most valuable commodity we have. As you get older, the time you have becomes more valuable, as you wonder how much time you have left to play with. Consider how you use your time. What time do you give to those around you who are important? How much of your time do you devote to your work? Is it too much, or too little? At one point I realised that I gave far too much of my precious time to my work – more time than I was getting paid for. Time that I could devote to my children or to thinking about how to use my time more effectively. Over time we pick up bad habits and rarely stop to evaluate if we are on the right path. So, dedicate some time to make sure you are spending it well. In the right places and with the people you love the most.

Don't let your mouth overload your back, say no to people. How often do we agree to do something we don't want to do? Just because we don't feel we can say no. Saying "no" is the greatest gift we can give ourselves, and we mustn't feel guilty when we use it. Practise saying no. Remember: You don't need to provide an excuse or give a reason for your decision. Just say NO. Saying no will create the space you need to say YES to the things that nourish you and make you feel good.

You are the average of the five people you spend most of your time with. Wow, really? Do the people you spend your time with give something to you, or do they drain your energy and zap your motivation? Carefully consider who you spend your time with. And yes, if that means letting go of people, then do it. Foster relationships with people who align with your personal values, who aspire to the same beliefs, who are positive and who bring out the best in you. Believe me, you won't regret it.

Random Acts of Kindness

Don't just learn how to earn, learn how to live. How good does it feel to do something special for someone? How good does it feel to give a good tip after you've received great service? How good does it feel to make someone's day? Giving provides you with a great feeling for the day. There are so many ways you can impact those around you and ultimately feel great about yourself.

Stop to lend a hand, let a stranger go in front of you at the checkout, buy a coffee for the person behind you in a queue or a homeless person on the street, leave a nice note on a co-worker's desk, send a nice text to a friend, give a compliment, call a family member, bring a treat to work, hold the door open for someone, let someone merge in front of you in traffic, leave a nice note in a library book. Or give a simple, powerful, and free gift: a smile!

Don't you feel good just reading those words of kind gestures? It feels 1,000 times greater when you do them, believe me.

But remember: Be kind to yourself. While you can do things for others all day, you won't feel good unless you do kind things for yourself too. Forgive yourself for a past mistake, cut off negative self-talk and remind yourself that you're amazing and doing the best you can.

Write Your Eulogy

A eulogy is written about a person after they have died. It reflects on the person's life and what they have accomplished. I stumbled across this as a personal development tool many years ago and found the whole idea both upsetting and ridiculous.

I remember the very difficult and painful task of writing a eulogy for my father just after he passed away. It remains to this day the most difficult passage I have ever had to write. And when the time came to read it out, I just couldn't get the words out. It was kindly read on my behalf, and to this day I wish I had found the strength to read it myself.

So why would I want to open this old wound and consider my own mortality? Morbid.

Well, I can only tell you that investing time to do this can give you an incredible sense of perspective and clarity. It can be the driving force that gives you that final push you need to take action. Yes, it might be painful, but you can decide to live a different life and make changes, to create the person you want to be remembered for.

The bad news is time flies; the good news is you're the pilot.

This time to do this is *now*, not in one year, or five years. Because one day it will be too late. Now if that doesn't make you feel motivated, then nothing will.

Writing your eulogy will help you follow your heart and accomplish the goals and dreams you long for. It can make you decide to live differently: to be a better mother, a better son or daughter, a better friend. It will help you live with purpose and a new awareness of the impact you have on this world and those around you.

Ultimately, this process helps you live a life with no regrets. And if this isn't possible, with few regrets. We've all heard stories about people's lives flashing before their eyes on their deathbeds and regretting their decisions or life choices. They have run out of time. Don't let time run away with you. Materialise a life where, on your deathbed, you are thankful for all you've achieved and for the love and positivity you've given to the world around you.

Before you embark on this exercise, I need to give you a word of warning. You need to be in a relatively "good place" to start out. It's no use doing this when you're at rock bottom and feel totally hopeless. Once you've built up a more positive mindset, you can now devote time to this. It will be hard. Take a long hard look at yourself with total honesty. Taking on board with complete transparency what you're about to realise about your life and how you live it can be transformational.

Firstly, you need to write about what your eulogy would say if you died today. Look back on your life, what would your close friends and family say about you and the life you had lived? What kind of person would they say you had been? What would they say was your greatest strength? What would they miss about you? I know this can be extremely painful, especially if you are honest with yourself. Don't hold back, no matter how painful this is. If needed, spend a few days pondering this and keep coming back to your writing.

Now is the good bit. Write your eulogy, but this is the one you *want* to be read after you leave this world. How do you want to be remembered? What do you want people to think and feel about you? What do you want them to say you were good at? What do you want people to admire about you? What lasting memories do you want people to remember about you for years to come? What do you want your grandchildren or great-grandchildren to be told about *you*? How will you be remembered? No one is going to stand up at your funeral and say, "She had an expensive couch and great shoes." Don't make life about stuff. Your legacy is the impact you leave on those around you.

I know this can also be painful, especially if you feel a hundred miles away from being this person. However, if you feel like that then you can make the change to strive to become the person you really want to be. The person you and your family deserve. If you don't go after what you want, you'll never have it. If you don't ask, the answer is always no. If you don't step forward, you are always in the same place. The only person you should be in competition with is the person you were yesterday. Make today and tomorrow the difference you want to see in your life.

The final part of this exercise is to explore what you need to stop, start, or continue doing in your life to realise your eulogy. This, in my view, is the most important part. You now know the impact you want to have on the world. How can you do this? Write a list with three columns, and name each column "Stop," "Start" or "Continue." Try to think of as many things you can list under each column. Maybe spend a few days compiling your list. I like to ponder on thoughts for a few days and usually come up with the best ideas doing this. Pick one or two things on each list that you want to 100%

commit to acting upon. These are simple steps you can take every day to live by the words you have written. Your eulogy.

When looking into our past we tend to discount the amazing things we have already done and the amazing impact we've had on people. To gain balance with this exercise, remember the impact you've already had on people is bigger than you think. Someone still giggles when they think of that funny thing you said. Someone still smiles when they think of the compliment you gave them. Someone silently admires you. The advice you give has made a difference for people. The support and love you've offered others has made someone's day. Your input and opinions have made someone think twice. You're not insignificant and forgotten.

Your existence makes a positive difference, whether you see it or not.

Conclusion

Now you are under no illusion as to how hard a divorce can be. You have learnt through my story the dark places that divorce can take you to. But you have also unearthed the strategies to unlock your future. You can and will now take control of your life, take back your power. You have discovered how to make the comeback of all comebacks.

Divorce is not the end; divorce is a delightful segue to self-power. Divorce is a rebirth, a second chance to be the woman and mother you've always wanted to be.

Your superpower for your future is that you fully know who you are, and you 100% know what you will and won't accept in your life. You know you don't *need* to depend on anyone for your personal growth and joy. *You* are the saviour of your own life, you are the superhero Mum that your children love and cherish. One day they will understand how amazing you are to have worked through the turmoil to discover a better life for them and you. They will look up to you in awe at the amazing person you became following your divorce. They will feel your close relationship and carry that blessing onto their relationships with their children. You have made the foundation for your family for years to come. You are strong, you are robust, you are tough, you are a formidable force. And you are filled with endless love and devotion for them.

There are so many experiences I have had post-divorce that I would never have had if I had continued in my loveless marriage year after year after year. Children deserve happy parents, not parents who put up with their lot, just because it seems like an easy road to travel. By reading this book you have made a great step to be different, to stand up for yourself and to start creating your new life.

They say that life is a journey, not a destination. This is so true, your life will forever be evolving, and you should always be curious and learning. You should always be discovering new things about yourself. And if you do this, with the knowledge you now have and the peace that you have found, you can face life's challenges with more ease. Because the very nature of life means that new challenges and difficulties will come up, how you navigate these now should be easier. But you need to continue doing the work. You need the resolve not to let it slip. You need to ensure that you are always working on yourself and looking for ways to improve.

Once you have battled with divorce and come out the other side, you have the right to know that you *can* and *will* be able to overcome anything that life throws at you. Because you see your own strength, you can pull on this inner hardiness when needed in different situations. You know you have an energy force within you that can overcome anything. You can stand alone or by the side of a new love in your life with strength and vigour.

You are the saviour and champion of your own life hereafter. Go out into this world, and work on your pre-, during, and post-divorce recovery. And believe me when I say that what lies ahead is worth fighting for.

And finally, as this book now comes to an end, the best piece of advice I can give you is to "keep on keeping on." My mum said this to me many times over the years, and it is solid and simple advice. A famous saying by Vincent Van Gogh brings this to life further: "Great things are done by a series of small things brought together." Even by doing one or two "small things," we are making progress. It has taken me many years to finally complete this book. And the *only* reason you are reading this now is that I have kept on going. Sometimes after a long break, I have continued to keep on going, many times over.

I have worked through the most difficult and painful months and even years of my life by "keeping on." Because what is the other option? I remember at my lowest point, when I no longer wanted to live, I found the strength to *keep on going*. Life will never be perfect; some people go through life without significant toil and struggle and that's wonderful. But for most people, it takes work. It takes strength to pick yourself up. It takes putting one foot in front of another so you can finally get to a good place. Only then do you have the foundation to build your happiness, hope and greatness.

For everyone who has experienced divorce, to all the amazing single mums and dads out there: I salute you. It is truly the hardest job going it alone in this world, bringing in the hard cash and caring for delicate hearts and minds – when at times you feel you're losing your own mind. Remember, it's hard to beat a person who never gives up!

So, keep on keeping on folks. This epic journey is now over for me as I write these last few words. There'll be more from me in my series of books in the near future. Because now that I've started writing, I'm not going to stop!

Much love to you all x

Ang

"One day you will tell your story of how you overcame what you went through, and it will be someone else's survival guide."
– Brene Brown

References

[1] McBride, Dr. Karly, Ph.D. "Help! I'm Divorcing a Narcissist", Psychology Today, Sussex Publishers, LLC, https://www.psychologytoday.com/intl/blog/the-legacy-distorted-love/201203/help-im-divorcing-narcissist

[2] Howton, Elizabeth. "Nearly Half the World Lives on Less than $5.50 a Day," *World Bank Group*, Washington, The World Bank, 2018, https://www.worldbank.org/en/news/press-release/2018/10/17/nearly-half-the-world-lives-on-less-than-550-a-day

[3] UK Finance, "Over half of those looking for love online vulnerable to romance scams." *UK Finance Limited trading as UK Finance*, 1 Angel Court, London, https://www.ukfinance.org.uk/press/press-releases/over-half-those-looking-love-online-vulnerable-romance-scams

[4] UK Finance, "Nearly 40 per cent of people looking for love online were asked for money." *UK Finance Limited trading as UK Finance*, 1 Angel Court, London, https://www.ukfinance.org.uk/press/press-releases/nearly-40-cent-people-looking-love-online-were-asked-money

[5] Byrne, Rhonda. *The Secret,* Australia, Atria Books/Beyond Words, 2006.

Printed in Great Britain
by Amazon